THE LETTERS OF MERCURIUS

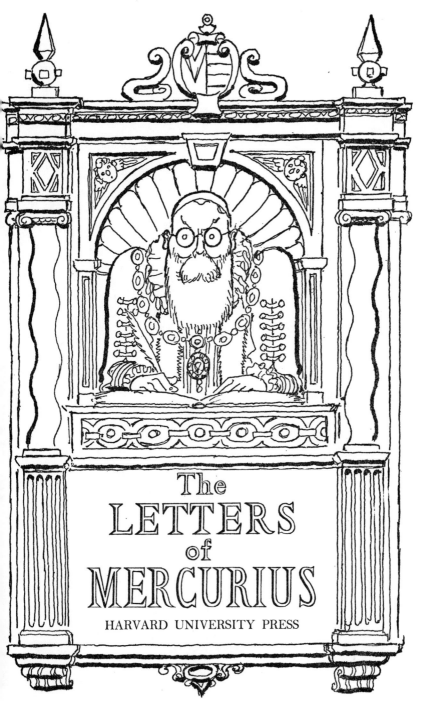

The
LETTERS
of
MERCURIUS

HARVARD UNIVERSITY PRESS

PREFACE

These letters, which have already become valuable documents of social and academic history, are here printed from the original manuscripts now in the possession of the well known professor at the London School of Economics, Mercurius Londiniensis. They have previously been printed in the *Spectator*, but unfortunately always from unauthorised and sometimes from imperfect copies. It has therefore seemed desirable to print the exact texts, in order at least to mitigate the embarrassment caused to the writers of the letters by that publication.

The writer of most of the letters, Mercurius Oxoniensis, is so well known to his friends in Oxford that there is no need to say anything about him here. As is apparent from his letters, he is a college tutor in one of the colleges in Turl Street: a bachelor, of declining years and uncertain health, somewhat old-fashioned in his views, as in his language, fond of his glass of port or hock, and teaches, *inter alia*, the *Politics* of Aristotle. He is slightly crotchety, but kept generally in good humour by his family circle and friends. Some of these are known to us from his letters, e.g. his sister Iris Oxoniensis, his college scout Ephraim Mudge, and his country host 'squire' Todhunter, whom we assume to be that well known rural character Euseby Todhunter M.F.H., of the Old Fox-Earth, Quainton, Bucks. In spite of all these clear indications, there is a remarkable uncertainty about Mercurius's identity and some very implausible conjectures have been put forward. To end all controversy, we are therefore publishing an authentic portrait of Mercurius by his friend Mr Osbert Lancaster.

The Editor is indebted to Mercurius Londiniensis for giving access to the original letters, and to Mercurius Oxoniensis for allowing them to be printed; also to Euphemia Edinensis for copyright permission in the case of the single letter from her late brother Mercurius Edinensis, whose sudden death from influenza early in 1970 has left a melancholy gap in the learned and lively society of Edinburgh.

Mercurius Oxoniensis, though otherwise punctilious, has never acquired the habit of dating his letters. They have therefore been printed with the date on which they were published in the *Spectator*. This provides a convenient *terminus ante quem*.

It only remains for the Editor to thank Mr Nigel Lawson, the then Editor of the *Spectator*, who has compounded for his audacity in printing unauthorised texts by his assistance in this authorised version; whereby his amicable relations with Mercurius Oxoniensis, once in jeopardy, have been fully restored.

September 1970

CONTENTS

Contents

THE LETTERS OF MERCURIUS

I

STUDENT STIRS

Mercurius Oxoniensis to Mercurius Londiniensis
15 November 1968

GOOD BROTHER LONDINIENSIS

Yours of the 28th *ultimi*, bearing news of the utter failure of the fanatiques' great demonstration in London[1], has brought good cheer to all loyall hearts in Oxon. This failure of their city friends has greatly abashed our university fanatiques too; of whose anticks 'tis now my turn to give you some accompt, both as a fair return for your civility and to encourage the honest party amongst you. But I will begin by telling you of their strength and disposition and then proceed to the heroicall acts which they have performed in the past week.

Know then that the fanatiques here are but few, and those gathered largely in two of our colleges, one old and one new, but both equally hideous: so true it is, as the philosophers say, that grace of body reflects grace of mind, and *vice versâ*. The first of these two colleges is Balliol coll., originally founded by a Scotchman, as a penance for murther, but not a penny paid by him (they being a parcimonious race), and since nurtured constantly in rebellion, having had one Wycliffe (a crabb'd heretique)

---

[1] The great London demonstration of Sunday 27 October 1968, organised by Mr Tariq Ali, was designed to begin the revolution and usher in the new society. It failed to do either.

I

as its Master, and his successors little better. The other is Nuffield coll., lately founded by a hugely rich mechanick, who thought thus to supply himself with ingeniose merchant-factors. But alas! 'twas scarce founded before it was coloniz'd from Balliol, whose then Master, the late lord Lindsay, being inward with the founder, cozened the old man into filling the place with young fry from his own spawning-bed. 'Tis now peopled with neoterick tub-preachers, who dignify themselves with sesquipedalian names, as psephologists, sociologists, etc.: *anglice* agitators.

From these two seminaries comes all the heresy that is now troubling this university; as indeed is manifest to whosoever walks the streets of Oxon. For the walls of Balliol coll. are today chalked from top to bottom with the canting slogans of the sect, all of them treasonable, most obscene, many illiterate, threatening destruction or perverse usage to loyall subjects. Indeed that whole coll. is now little other than an extroverted privy-house: the scribblings which there, through shame, are writ inwardly being here shamelessly publish'd to the world. Elsewhere in the university such writings are to be found, but scattered; and 'tis likely they are all done by vagrant Balliol men; for the idiom is the same, and other colls., though infected, still retain some reliques of publick decency.

Here let me say that, save in Balliol coll., of which there is no hope, having been always a nest of sedition, 'twould be easy to stop the rot, were it not for a tribe of young Fellows, mostly bred in Balliol or Nuffield, if not both, who, after having sucked in the rank vapour of those places, have been planted out in more wholesome ground, to teach those new-fangled subjects which drowsy guardians have suffered to be added to our good old *trivium* and *quadrivium*; and the sooner they are brought to order, by lopping their tainted branches and spraying their stumps with a good drench of sound doctrine, the better we shall all thrive.

The fanatiques also print every week a pamphlet called *Cherwell*, which some think founded in memory of my lord Cherwell, lately deceased. If so, it has sadly declined since his time, his Lordship having been always a loyall subject, a high-flyer for legitimacy, divine right and privilege of peers. This rag is now writ in the same style as the wall-scribblings on Balliol coll., and most probably by the same people: for otherwise 'tis hardly to be believed that there are ninnies enough to go round. 'Tis the organ of their party, like your *Black Dwarf*, which I am glad to learn is now ailing and suspended. It gives them their orders, which they, being very sheep, do obey.

On the failure of your gyant demonstration in London, the fanatiques here were mightily cast down and there was at first much lamentation, breast-beating and calls to repentance; but soon they pluckt up courage, and this aforesaid pamphlet summoned them to bury the memory of that discomfiture by performing some new and signall feat of arms, *viz*: to besiege All-soules coll., which, having no undergraduates to defend it, they thought a rich prize, easily taken; besides that there was within it one Dummett, a rogue Wykehamist, upon whom, like Rahab the harlot, they thought that they could rely. So for three days they surrounded the college, bearing furious placards and a banner proclaiming 'em to be Oxon Revolutionary Students. But the college porters, a sound and orthodox race of men, shut fast the gates and

3

let none in or out, save only Dr Rowse, who for a moment, as 'tis reported, appeared at the gate *more Romano* to abuse the enemy: which he did right well, and naturally. The Warden, Master Sparrow, showed himself a stout captain on this occasion. Deserting his Sotadean studies, and foregoing his equestrian exercise, which he takes every week for his health, he manned the battlements, refused all parley, and even, in a sortie (as 'tis said), captured the enemy banner; which next day, under a flag of truce, was civilly returned (but with some secret changes in the inscription). On the third day, the effects of the siege began to be felt in the coll., insomuch as the Fellows of All-soules, who are accustomed to live delicately (too delicately, as some say), were happy to share an ass's head for their dinner, and a fourth part of a cab of dove's dung for their dessert: which was all the Gaudy they had this year. But then suddenly, hearing a meer rumour that a relieving army was on its way from Christ-church or Trinity (two loyall colls., much abused for their loyalty), the fanatiques broke up and, after an unseemly attempt to intrude into the Congregation House, where Mr Vice-chancellour, in a panick, was pushing through some unnecessary bill of appeasement, they dispersed and have not since been seen, and the kitchens of All-soules coll. have been fully replenished.

After this rebuff, the fanatiques are trying a new course. Through their weekly pamphlet they are now seeking to disaffect the college porters, as the first obstacle to their invasion of other colls., and through their dupes in the university they are clamouring for controul over teaching, lest the ingenuous young should be taught to think for themselves, and over discipline, lest their ringleaders

4

should at any time be silenced or sent away; all of which they put in such virtuous, innocent language that many are cozened by them; but none so gullible as those who wish to be gulled; of which we have too many.

This then, good friend Londiniensis, is the sum of the goings-on in Oxon, which must surely be of great encouragement to you in London. For believe me, there is nothing in all these stirs of callow students but what, by a timely show of firmness and rationality, could be totally dissipated; as all our loyall, tax-paying citizens here readily agree, who would gladly see justice done and a gallows erected, as by statute allowed, at Magdalen Bridge, had our academicall governours but the courage which the times require and which we mere centurions in the Republick of Letters would gladly give 'em. But these are yielding times and few are willing to see whither all this appeasement will lead us: 'tis easier for college drones to buzz with the hive and make a virtue of their harmony than, by independency, to change the tune and be thought excentrique. On which note, good brother Londiniensis, I bid you farewell.

Your loving brother to serve you,
MERCURIUS OXONIENSIS

P.S. 'Tis just reported that there has been a revolution in Balliol coll., and that the Master, Dr Hill, has been hanged in his doctor's robes by the fanatiques, whom he once led, but who have now elevated one Cobb, a Ranter, in his place. The report is as yet unconfirmed, but 'tis very plausible, and so not to be discounted.

II

HOW MASTER FULLER WON THE DAY

Mercurius Oxoniensis to Mercurius Londiniensis
29 November 1968

Good brother Londiniensis

I have stayed my pen this se'nnight till I might report to you the issue of our great Poetry contest; which is now over, and your Mr Roy Fuller, the attorney, crowned victor, to the great satisfaction of all who love the Muses. But before coming to that I must cleer some doubts left in the postscript of my last letter, concerning student stirs.

What I writ about the revolution in Balliol coll. is, alas, too true. The late Master was hustled to his grave at midnight, very obscurely: no Heads of Houses present, as fearing the like treatment; but the Warden of All-soules, who since the siege of his coll. has kept close in his lodgings (now new-fortified), is busy about a Latin epitaph. The Proctors have forgiven the young men who hanged their Master, as doubtless ignorant of the statutes against murther. Master Cobb, the Ranter, now rules the roast in that coll., at least until he shall dissent from the fanatiques, who will then haply treat him likewise; but meanwhile he trots to their tune, as will appear, even in this matter of the Poetry Chair.

For of late the undergraduates have claimed a voice in this election, as in all else. They complain that since 'tis they who must listen to the Professor's lectures, they should in justice choose him rather than submit to one imposed upon 'em by the cabals of their seniors; which complaint, though of a piece with their epidemick insolency, would have some colour of reason to it, were their own motives any purer. So they presumed to have their own election and then, through their *coryphaeus* Cobb, entered their chosen candidate for our race. But here their reason deserted 'em, for the candidate they put forward was one Eugenius Eutychianus[1], a Tartar from Muscovy, who speaks no English, save what jargon he may have picked up in the Antipodes (for his masters send him abroad as a decoy-duck), and whose poems are all locked up in the Sclavonian language, unknown to his silly patrons. But *omne ignotum pro magnifico*, and so the young geese have run cackling after this Muscovy-duck, and Master Cobb, an old gander, creaks behind 'em.

This Eugenius, I hear, is a good patriot but a mighty dissembler, who abroad declaims odes to Liberty but at home writes panegyricks on the conquest of Bohemia and diatribes against the domestick enemies of his Prince; which gets him credit both here and there. Having pitched upon him, his promoters put forth to all resident Masters of Arts a peremptory paper, as from 700 senior and junior gownsmen (but no names given), bidding 'em elect their Eugenius or the whole Academy should stand convicted before the world of vulgar and narrow patriotism: which, it seems, is commendable only in a Muscovite. But now they are all routed and we shall hear no more of this Children's Crusade.

---

[1] i.e., in the vulgar tongue, Evgeny Yevtuchenko, the Russian poet.

The Letters of Mercurius

There have been other motions no less excentrique. There was a jovial Welsh harpist who hath writ (like the Tartar) only in his own tongue and who, 'twas thought, might pick up a few votes in Jesus coll., besides what he brought with him in a merry symposiack party. Also a young man from Newcastle-upon-Tyne, the first in the field, who farts in Pindarick metre, and a thrasonicall young upstart from the Plantations who as yet hath not even farted (but that climate breeds impertinency). Some of the preciser sort among us would find means to exclude such as these two, as degrading our honourable chair into a close-stool; but 'tis not necessary: they exclude themselves on polling day, as the score testifies. There was one Scotchman, from Edinburgh, who intruded himself into this contest, and for whom not one vote was cast, not even by his own nominators, who, it seems, had repented of their nomination, thus declaring no less their own levity than his insufficiency.

The great challenger was our own Mistress Starkie of Somerville coll., who, having managed many such elections in the past fifteen years, has by now built up an engine thought invincible. She has long been a beacon of light (flickering, not steady) in that coll., otherwise a dim place. She has bred up many pupills, whom she has fired with zeal for liberty, if not disorder, and by her agitating genius (she is an Hibernian, from Donegall) and her free hospitality (an unlicensed poteen-still in her bedroom), she has an army at her command, which she directs at will, sometimes for this or that candidate, sometimes, it seems, for diversion only, to make a noise. This time, her first candidate, Master Blunden, having left his post by reason of bodily infirmity, she, as a stout generall,

8

sprang into the breach and rallied her broken cohorts with drum and trumpet. And indeed 'twas a brave sight to see her enter the lists with 227 supporters scratched together from bogs and nunneries; and all *in terrorem* only, for two would have sufficed, and few of these raw kerne and galloglass would be there at the fight.

Having thus declared war, she waged it briskly, setting up a *scriptorium* of busy, pragmaticall letter-writers to sollicit votes; but sometimes, the pace being too hard for them all, she would herself descend into the arena; which, through lack of good order at headquarters, bred confusion. One grave doctor received two letters of sollicitation, one from the chief scribe, explaining that the *generalissima* was too modest to write in her own behalf, the other from the *generalissima* herself, her scribes being all now (as she thought) disabled by writer's cramp. She set agents awork in your city too, not graduates but ladies of ease and fashion, who have been very active, advising their academick friends. But this Amazonian strategy has not always prospered, some of our senatours supposing that they have minds, as well as votes, of their own and can regulate the one by the other, without being whipt to the poll by rattle-pated Sempronias in Kensington.

And here I cannot but note that 'twas an error to appear in such strength at the beginning. 'Tis votes, not nominations, that win the day, and so extravagant a defiance quickens even us old college tortoises into opposite motion. Besides, a good jockey whips not his nag in the first furlong. 'Twould have been better to go to work more quietly than to make such a din and do Master Fuller's work for him, who had but to sit still and be carried, by his modesty and merits, to victory. With which sound morall reflexion I leave you, good brother Londiniensis, till events here in Oxon shall again sharpen my nib; when I shall not fail to advertize you.

Your loving brother to serve you,

MERCURIUS OXONIENSIS

III

NEWS FROM OXON

Mercurius Oxoniensis to Mercurius Londiniensis
13 December 1968

GOOD BROTHER LONDINIENSIS

I had not meant to trouble you with another letter so soon, especially at this season, when we poor college moles can scarce gnaw our way through the solid mounds of rubbish daily shovelled over us from the publick schools. But Master Lawson, with whom I lately exchanged a tankard of ale at the ordinary, tells me that there is a matter upon which you particularly desire to be informed, *viz*: our great victory in the long warre of the Christ-church Meadow. In which your request I would gladly pleasure you, but I must beg you to wait another se'nnight, till I have discharged two more immediate duties. For first, I must do what I can to stuff the sons of my old friends into my coll. (a task which becomes harder, and they duller each year), and secondly, I must show myself at a brace of those college feasts, of which Master Montefiore, of Cambridge (*sed ex Cantabrigia semper aliquid novi*), would have us deprived, so that our roasted pheasants and vintage port-wine may be shipped abroad to Hindoos and Hottentots, to give 'em colick[1]. For this necessary delay, there-

---

[1] This shocking proposal was actually made by the Revd. Hugh Montefiore, now Bishop of Kingston-on-Thames, in a sermon in Great Saint Mary's Church, Cambridge.

fore, I pray you excuse me; and in the mean time I shall despatch some small matters left hanging from my last letter.

The student stirs are now over, dead of their own folly even before they were interrupted by the Christmas dispersal. Since the siege of All-soules coll. was so ignominiously raised, there was nothing the fanatiques could do without incurring universal ridicule; and when the blackamoor who led 'em had been properly snibbed for his impertinency by the Warden of Rhodes House, and their great scribbler, for his gross plebeian vulgarity, had been silenced by one snort from the Warden of Wadham, they were all so cast down that their very rag, *Cherwell*, died away prematurely, in the seventh week of term, for lack of matter. So cleer it is that one stout word of command would long since have settled all this sawciness:

> *Hi motus animorum atque haec certamina tanta*
> *Pulveris exigui jactu compressa quiescunt.*

Of the revolution in Balliol coll. we have no certain news since the sudden deposition of Master Cobb, the Ranter; but some pathetick letters from him have been conveyed out of that coll. and are being passed from hand to hand. One of them came to Master Lawson, who has printed it[1]. It seems that the poor Ranter is now held close prisoner by the fanatiques, who threaten to try him, by summary *junto*, and will no doubt presently turn him off, like his precursor; but what will follow no man knows. Some think that the creditors of the college, being now impatient, will intermeddle and impose that great oeconomist my lord Balogh as Master, with increased

---

[1] In the *Spectator* 6 December 1968.

powers and a troop of musqueteers from the county militia (if not Hungarian hussars) to keep him in office. Otherwise, the fanatiques will be starved of victuals, the Oxon tradesmen having stopt all credit, and they having by now emptied all the bottles in the cellar (which in that coll. are of ginger-beer only).

The great Poetry contest is now no longer questioned. My lord Thomson's man from the Antipodes, who came to trumpet the victory of his fellow-bigot, the Tartar Eugenius, has now slunk back home to correct his weak thoughts, leaving us all bewildered by this strange enlistment[1]. The Scotchman who obtained no votes at all is publishing letters to assure us that the fault is in the voters and that a more equall method of voting would have carried him in triumph into the chair. Meanwhile he boasts of the high fees which he has pocketed by indecently exposing himself on the gogglebox during the contest; which sufficiently shows the quality of his service to the Muses. Only Mistress Starkie has not yet digested her defeat. She has sent out publick letters in all directions, and followed 'em up with hot postcards (Master Lawson showed me one over the second tankard), demanding redress against (*inter alios*) the Regius History Professor who, it seems, has tweaked her tail in some way, and against whom she now threatens to vindicate her affronted honour by some signall act, yet to be declared.[2]

---

[1] The cause of Mr Yevtuchenko was vigorously promoted in the *Sunday Times* both by that paper's Moscow correspondent, Edmund Stevens, and by the Australian communist Frank Hardy, who came specially to London to press it.

[2] Dr Enid Starkie had taken exception to a letter from Professor H. R. Trevor-Roper concerning the contest for the chair of poetry, printed in the *Spectator* 15 November 1968.

'Tis presumed by most that (the law being not clear on her side) she will call upon one of her 227 champions to challenge the professor to a duel in Port Meadow (the usual place for such encounters); but whom she will call, we as yet know not. If fire-arms be used, 'tis supposed she will employ her fellow-Hibernian, my lord Longford: a martiall earl who carries in his bottom honourable wounds from the late warre (a bosh-shot from the Christchurch cook while exercising with the Home Guard, *anno* 1940); but he being an erratick marksman (his mind always on higher things), the lady may resort to spirituall arms, as more efficacious. These will doubtless be wielded for her by Father Corbishley, a subtile Jesuit who knows a popish trick or two and has bewitched many to serve his deep designs (as the Bishop of —— and Master —— in the matter of St Clare: but this *inter nos*). There are some of us here who would gladly see that proud piece of a professor silenced, by whatever means; and I among 'em. So, if the earl shoots straight, or the Jesuit conjures well with his hocus-pocus and his holy-water, you may count on me for a tart epitaph in my next letter.

Thus much only will I send you this se'nnight, good brother Londiniensis; but when these college feasts are over, and the boyes stuff'd in, I shall send you, as you desire, a full accompt of our great warre against the Roadhogs, together with some arcane details hitherto prudently withheld and some useful morall reflexions, which you may haply apply in your own affairs; in which you can always expect good will and firm counsell from

your loving brother to serve you,
MERCURIUS OXONIENSIS

IV

HOW VIRTUE TRIUMPHED OVER PROGRESS

Mercurius Oxoniensis to Mercurius Londiniensis

20 December 1968

GOOD BROTHER LONDINIENSIS

I hear no more as yet of Mistress Starkie's great duel, and so I go straight to the main matter: the long warre (longer than the warre of Troy) in which now, it seems, we have at last defeated those Road-hogs that would have driven a turnpike road through our Christ-church Meadow.

You must know that this Meadow, which they describe as a mere waste marsh, ripe for development, and we as an oasis of rustick peace in our urban *Pandaemonium*, is a great field, like your Hyde Park, betwixt Christ-church and the river, bounded by walks and trees (some of them exotique), which Christ-church, a rich coll., has always maintained at its own expense for the refreshment of all citizens of Oxon, except such as are of improper character, push hand-carts, or wear ragged or very dirty clothes: a *proviso* now (save in the matter of hand-carts) lamentably disregarded. Some pragmaticall busybodies in the town have long clamoured for a road through this Meadow. They allege publickly that it would be a great relief to the High-street, drawing away the stink and noise and discharging it elsewhere; and they add (but privately, among themselves only) that it would also be a swipe in the eye to a rich proud college. But 'twas not till 1956, when the late Master Alexander Smith, Warden of New coll., was Vice-chancellour, that such novelties received any inlet into the university, which till then (whether through good sense or naturall torpor) had been content not to tickle a sleeping dog. But Master Smith, who had a twitching finger, soon changed all that.

This Master Smith was Vice-chancellour by accident, being at the time of his elevation already past the age of retirement. But his coll., wishing to soften some precedent misfortune, and to reward his universal affability, voted to continue him in office as Warden, and so, by seniority (Buggins' turn), bestowed him on the university as Vice-chancellour; in which new office he resolved to savour his triumph, and so set out, in great haste (as old men do who come late to power), to eternize his reign by some memorable disturbance of Nature. He was a man of gothick taste, which heretofore he had been unable to express; for although he had set out to re-modell the windows of his own coll., he had been stopt by the Fellows after the first window, which remains as his monument there (Smith's Folly). So now, being Vice-chancellour, he hoped to gratify this taste in a larger theatre; and since he was endowed with a bold spirit and an exalted fancy and an indefatigable, bewitching tongue, he drew many after him.

His design was to convert the whole High-street into a cobbled *piazza*, open only to foot-walkers, sandwich-men, hot-dog-vendors, morris-dancers, etc., and to those hand-carts which the Dean of Christ-church had excluded from the Meadow; for which purpose he would seal up the ends of the High-street with posts and chains and divert all the other stinking traffique into the Meadow, along a new road to be built under the Dean's nose. To this end he courted the city, already half won; ventilated his *piazza* to the other colls. in the High-street, offering them a new golden age of peace and quietude; ran up to London to inveigle Her Majesty's minister (Master Duncan Sandys, a Magdalen man) into his scheme; and by some sleight of hand in committees (avoiding a direct vote in Congregation), had it put out that the whole university joined the city in petitioning her Majesty to bestow upon us a Meadow Road.

His great ally in all this was his former pupill, Master Sparrow, Warden of All-soules coll., who has much free time at his disposal (no undergraduates in that delicious place), and who was himself much taken by the plan, being greatly distracted from his refined and subtile machinations by the noise and stink of the traffique in the High-street (*vide* on this the exquisite poem by Master Osbert Lancaster, published at that time in the *Spectator*, and beginning

> Hark, hark, the traffique rouls
> Past the Warden of All-soules, *etc.*)

This Master Sparrow would hop often up to London and make interest in the Athenaeum, Albany, Beefsteak Club, and suchlike places, and would draft neat lawyerlike arguments in which to entangle the honest party while Master Vice-chancellour swept forward, at long strides, intoxicated, like a sleep-walker, in a gothick trance, with Her Majesty's Minister and Master Mayor and the City Counsellours (a bare quorum of 'em) running after him, clapping their hands and crying, in unison, 'A Meadow Road! A Meadow Road!'

Of course 'twas but an empty slogan, framed to unite 'em, for beyond the bare words they agreed in nothing, nor looked past their own noses. The City Counsellours would not say where they would drive their road, once it was through the Meadow, lest they should lose the votes of those whose houses they would pull down, and the High-street colls. would not see that their *piazza* was but an aëry *chimaera*, for the City took care never to agree to it. But whenever the honest party hinted at these difficulties, they all shut their eyes and sang out 'A Meadow Road! A Meadow Road!' as if that were a charm to exorcise impossibilities; and sometimes they changed their tune and said gravely that their Meadow Road would be a thing of beauty, and that they would line it with topiary bushes clipped in the shape of Master Vice-chancellour and Master Mayor *et al.*, and emblematick flower-beds in red, white and blue, and plastick gnomes and gyant stone toadstools, and God wot what not, to teach us poor rusticks true taste, etc. etc.

At this the Meadow colls. got together and Christ-church, as the most concerned, tweaked a string in the metropolis, and a debate was launched in the House of Peers, and many excellent speeches made, especially by the hereditary peers, most of whom had spent a brief time at Christ-church and had kindly memories of the Meadow, in which they had breathed their unlicenced greyhounds, beagles, whippets, etc. (and perhaps tumbled a bird or two). But all came to nothing, the government peers fearing to risk their coronets by defying what was called The Voice of People—though it was but the voice of Master Vice-chancellour and Master Warden Sparrow and a few tradesmen, ingeniosely amplified; and their

Lordships might as well have blown themselves up in a good cause as wait to be snuffed out, as now seems likely, without a squeak, in no cause at all. So the Road-hogs prevailed, and the government told the City to go on boldly and build their road.

About this time Nicolas, Grand Prince of Muscovy, finding himself opposed by his Boyars[1], and learning that, in Oxon, Master Vice-chancellour had diddled all his opponents, came over and waited humbly on Master Vice-chancellour, who gave him good advice (of which he was always liberall); and on his return to his own country, the Prince invited Master Vice-chancellour thither as his own guest, in great state. But alas, this visit, which marked the apogee of Master Vice-chancellour's royall progress (for he had already bestowed doctorates, *honoris causa*, on the King of Sweden and the Emperour of Aethiopia), was also the procatarctick cause of his decline. For in Muscovy (a dirty place) he caught the itch, and sickened, and on his return home had to abdicate his office, and soon afterwards died, to the unfeigned grief of all men, of whatever party: for he was a man of high spirit and winning manners, though somewhat over-zealous and arbitrary in his proceedings and obstinate in his gothick fantasy. After his return, the Prince of Muscovy applied the advice he had given and soon diddled the Boyars, dismissing them from office and sending them away, some to manage manufactories in the country, some to exile in Mongolia, etc. In Oxon, the new Vice-chancellour being Sir John Masterman, a Christ-church man, the mantle of Master Smith now fell on Master

---

[1] In 1957 Nikita Krushchev found himself opposed by an 'Anti-Party Group' in the Russian Politburo; whom he outmanoeuvred and deposed.

Warden Sparrow, who (as he thought) had but to wear it and sit and fiddle till the ripe fruit of victory should drop into his lap.

For now it seemed that all was over, and nothing left for the friends of the Meadow but to keen over the desolation thereof. For the survayors began to measure the Meadow, this way and that, carving it up in their minds, and the contractors to sniff the spoils, and although good men protested, and totted up figures, and Sir Roy Harrod (the great oeconomist), with marvellous eloquence, urged them at least to sink their road underground, in a tunnel (so that they might all be drowned in it, at floodtime), yet the Road-hogs did but laugh at them, or pilloried them as enemies of Progress and of the People, and so cowed 'em into silence. And Christ-church in particular, for its gallantry and civick spirit, was lampooned, as if it were a crime to be rich, or to stand alone, guarding the interests of beauty and of the publick, against those Gadarene road-hogs who stampeded, grunting identicall grunts, down the broad way which leads to destruction. And even the best friends of that coll., great peers and cabinet counsellours, urged 'em to yield; for, said they, these are yielding times, 'tis best to be with it, to go with the herd; otherwise (besides the cost of it) we shall all be branded as heretiques, enemies of Progress, and of Master Warden Sparrow, and of the People.

Nevertheless, that great coll. was not deflected from its purpose but stood firm, sustained by the other Meadow colleges and by divers bold spirits in the university. These together brought the matter into Congregation (whence Master Smith had always excluded it) and there caused the true mind of the university to be declared. They also fee'd learned counsell, at huge expense, and fought inch by inch, and ensnared opposing learned counsell into long, labyrinthine disputations, so that all men marvelled at their virtuosity and the Publick Inquests became publick entertainments, like pantomimes or horse-races or raree-shows; and thus they held out till the government of the city had changed, and of the country too, and new survays were made, and all the old summs were shown to be wrong, and a new arithmetique was brought in, and a new philosophy, and little by little the light dawned in men's minds, and the very survayors imployed by the city have now reported that a Meadow Road is not needed, nay is flat contrary to Scripture, Aristotle and right reason.

So you see, good brother Londiniensis, how virtue and sound sense can triumph, even in these degenerate days, if we do but stand fast till the epidemick folly passes, as it surely will; for the giddy multitude follows the fashion, and 'tis our duty, as guardians of ingenuous youth, not to yield to it, but *stare super antiquas vias*; which I trust will be our New Year's resolve. Till when I wish you and your lady Mercuria and all your household a merry Christmas, far from student stirs and election cabals, and untroubled by these prolix letters of mine. For I, being a batchelour, shall this week break covert from Oxon, and having shaken off my pursuers, who are now hot on my brush, seeking to rip me open and cut off my mask, I shall go safely to ground with my good friend squire Todhunter at Quainton, with whom I commonly enjoy my delitescency and sweet otiums. But there, as always, I shall remain
your loving brother to serve you,
MERCURIUS OXONIENSIS

V

A BRIEF LIFE

Mercurius Oxoniensis to Mercurius Londiniensis
[undated]

G OOD BROTHER L ONDINIENSIS

Your letter of 25 *ultimi*, wherein you ask me whether to lay out 35 shillings on this new life of our common friend, the late Master Robin Dundas,[1] of Christ-church and Parson's Pleasure, comes very timely to hand. For by the very same post I received, from Master John Aubrey F.R.S., a brief life of the same worthy collegian, which he has writ (as he tells me) for a projected revision, up to our own time, of Master Antony Wood of Merton coll. his *Athenae Oxonienses*. Master Aubrey writes further that he has many other such pieces already prepared for that purpose, which he keeps under close lock and key, for good reason; but this he has released, for you and me only, as being known friends of that good old man. Which brief life I enclose herewith, and thus excuse myself (being busy about our college Gaudy) for an even briefer letter, and subscribe myself

your loving brother to serve you,

M ERCURIUS O XONIENSIS

Enclosure[2]

---

[1] *D, Portrait of a Don.*
[2] The enclosure is printed as an Appendix.

VI

ON THE THOUGHTS OF MASTER HART

Mercurius Oxoniensis to Mercurius Londiniensis

7 June 1969

Good brother Londiniensis

I have not troubled you with my papers these last weeks, lest I should seem to insult your broils by boasting of our peace; for indeed, since our fanatiques were laughed off the stage in November last, and our Road-hogs routed by the heroicall resistance of the Christ-church men, this place has enjoyed such tranquillity as befits the temple of Apollo and the Muses. Even Balliol coll. is now clean, at least on the outside, which is all that honest men look on; and save in Brazen-nose Lane (a dark pissing-alley betwixt that coll. and Exeter coll.), I find no wall-scribblings left in the whole university. But how long this virtue will last, a wise man will not prognosticate.

For now has come forth the long bruited Report of our Verulamius (for he is both jurist and philosopher), Master Hart, late Professor of Law, an ingeniose and learned man. He was set awork a year since, with a few others of less note, to discover, by interrogatories and otherwise, whether the young men had any just grievance, either in doctrine or in discipline, and to propound remedies; and now concludes, very justly, that they have none, but 'tis all mere smoak. For none of them has been sent away, save by temporary rustication, nor fined more than the charge of a few tankards of ale at the ordinary, and that on good grounds: to such laxity are we come. Howsoever, Master Hart has not stopped here, but, to show his philosophy, has covered 200 pages, in *octavo*, with judicious reflexions, excellently writ[1]; which, though misliked by some as too yielding, have damped the more factious spirits and much relieved such of us poor college tortoises as are in no great hurry for change.

Briefly, Master Hart explodes all the arguments of the enemy by denying any necessary correspondency betwixt the modell of a commonwealth and the modell of an university within that commonwealth; so that even if (*quod Deus avortat*) we should sink to a parity in the former, we must still maintain a hierarchy in the latter. This, as you can conceive, has marvellously enraged the fanatiques, whose whole aëry fabrick is raised on a clean contrary bottom. But none now cares what they say; and since they refused to testify to the Committee (as being but a device to caulk the rotten hulk of the university, which they reckoned, with their squeaking nibs, to pierce and sink), 'tis now too late for them to start twittering, for we are all weary of them.

These therefore being left aside (or rather, thrust contemptuously into an Appendix), 'tis to the busy-bodies among the other students that Master Hart addresses himself, offering 'em a release from discipline and a voice in doctrine if they will but send deputies to sit on such boards and committees as he will frame for them; which will no doubt be infinitely taedious to all of us, and so clog the machine, that all our business will gradually be

[1]*University of Oxford: Report of the Committee on relations with junior members*, by H. L. A. Hart; OUP, May 1969.

conglutinated and come to a stop, and so, in the end, provide the in-let to some new tyranny.

Nevertheless, even here, the young men are not to have all their desires. For whereas they have flown high, and would perch and chatter on the topmost tribunals, in order (as they say) to learn the art of government, which they declare to be an empiricall, not a theoreticall art, and part of their necessary instruction as citizens of the Commonwealth, our Master Hart hath snibbed them sharply, reminding them that they come not hither to study our cabals and juntos but to learn piety, letters and good manners, which too many of them want. So, although he will allow 'em to run free, he will clip their wings, and their talons too; and while they may have a part in making of laws for themselves (thus depriving the Proctors of a part of their jurisdiction), there is to be a stiff statute forbidding 'em to daub walls or occupy publick buildings or interrupt professors; which for the past 800 years, when the young were civilly bred up, had never been thought necessary.

These propositions of Master Hart have caused much bumbling in our college hives, but indistinct, as of wasps or drones. The fanatiques buzz high and shrill, as knowing not what to do next. The other students humm busily and affect a grave air, as being already senatours in embryo, although there are, thank God, a few gay sparks still, to make merry at them. Our high tables likewise (which are now crowded with giggling girls in lewd skirts) are divided betwixt young ninnies, crying for novelties, and old gellies, quaking and yielding to them; all which is very taedious to us loyall subjects who, having disputed on Aristotle all day, come thither at night rather for port-

wine and rationall conversation than for further conten-
tion about Master Hart and his Report.

However, all is not yet over. Our two antient universities, as my lord Robbins has tartly observed[1], are ill-
framed gothick bodies which long freedom hath made
sawcy: they are not well-regulated, disciplined modells
like your new School of Oeconomicks which jumps so
instantly to obey his Lordship's commands. Master Hart
may propound, but 'tis for Hebdomadall Councill and the
Colleges and Congregation to dissect and debate his
propositions; and before we have heard all the witty,
inveigling speeches of Master Professor Beloff, Master
Cooper of Trinity coll., Master Warden Sparrow, and
other our academicall oratours, who knows but the
fashion among the young (being marvellous flighty) will
have changed? Our good friend Mercurius Cantabrigiensis tells me that already there the loyall young sparks are
reviving and may soon light a fire that will burn up all this
mundungus (and toast the bottoms of some seniors too);
and I am in hopes that, ere long, our own poor Gadarene
pigs may swerve back to their allegiance, though at the
brink, leaving only their besotted young swineherds, who
must needs show off their witt and their long legs by
trotting out in front of them, to tumble into the sea and be
choak'd; whose fate, being fully deserved, shall not be
much lamented by

your loving brother to serve you

MERCURIUS OXONIENSIS

[1] Lord Robbins, Chairman of the Governors of the London School of
Economics, in his Report on Higher Education (1963), saw fit to censure
Oxford and Cambridge for their anomalous structure—i.e. for differing from
L.S.E. By 1969 they felt fortunate in so differing.

P.S. Since I writ this letter, Master Hart's Report has been anatomiz'd, very querulously, in our domestick gazette, the *Oxford Magazine*. The author (as I am advertized) is a pragmaticall undergraduate of Oriel coll., who has come hither from some seminary of disaffection in the American plantations; as is clear from his style, being illiterate. 'Tis pity his coll. here could not furnish him with better tutors.

VII

ON A DOMESTICK TRAGEDY, etc.

Iris Oxoniensis to Mercuria Londiniensis

21 June 1969

Loving sister Mercuria

'Tis a sad office I must perform in writing to you this day, for my poor brother, your husband's old friend and fellow-collegian Mercurius Oxoniensis, is even now in Dr Radcliffe's Infirmary, very feverish and on no account to be troubled with the writing of letters. He is sick of a crack'd pate, which he acquired last Saturday evening from a fully charg'd wine-bottle, which, being tost casually out of a window in Lincoln coll. while he was scrutinizing the wall-scribblings in Brazen-nose lane, hit him plumb on the head; so that truly, as he says, he was well-nigh killed as a witness to the truth, and should be included in the next edition of the late Master Foxe's Book of Martyrs. He is now in a very low condition and has but one consolation, viz: that the projectile was, on examination, found to be a champagne-bottle, which (he says) argues that some at least of the young men are sound and do not waste the hours proper to conviviality in devizing aëry committees and seeking to participate in the business of their betters. 'Why, sister', he cry'd out, as good old Nurse Bedpan applied the plaister to his skull, 'do but think! Had there still been wall-scribblings on Balliol coll., I might have been laid out by a copper-

28

bottom'd cocoa-urn, or a firkin of distill'd water, or a volume of my lord Lindsay's Meditations, revised, bowdleriz'd and annotated by the now Master (whoever he may be): which would be a shameful end for an establish'd tutor and fellow of a college'. And at that mere thought he fell into a melancholy, very piteous to behold.

This domestick tragedy being reported to me on Sunday morning, as I was returning from parson Trulliber's sermon (which was on Elisha and the bears, very aptly applied to the insolency of our modern youth), I flew up from the country, and found poor Mercurius very weak, though much cheer'd by an armful of red roses, newly sent to console him by Mistress Starkie; which was very handsomely done and shows her to be a true lady. He lamented, very dismally, the restraints which this sad accident had put upon him; as, first, his inability to write to you about the new degree in Sociology and Sawciness which the Provost of King's coll. and his swinging crew have carried at Cambridge against the gallant opposition of the Master of Jesus coll. and others, concerning which he had just received a long letter from our friend Mercurius Cantabrigiensis, full of pithy observations; and, secondly, the impossibility of attending a great drinking-party at which all our young witts were to celebrate the knighting of Master Weidenfeld, who publishes their trash for 'em; and where he had hoped, by patient listening, to pick up (from my lord Balogh and others) some useful intelligence.

So much for his (and your) loss through that misdirected bottle. But for me this accident has a nearer consequence. For having reckoned on being taken by my good brother to Master Vice-chancellour's grand garden party in St John's coll. next Wednesday, I had but lately stretch'd my purse to buy a new hat, very modish, with goose-feathers in it and a cluster of grapes, marvellous lifelike, hanging over the brim of it, to show myself off to the Chancellour and *beau monde* of the university. Which hope is now altogether dash'd, unless I can find some good-natured batchelour (as Master Felix Markham of Hertford coll.; or Sir R. Syme, if he be not abroad, as usual, administering the Republick of Letters), under whose protection I may be able to insinuate myself into that assembly. But alas! 'tis too probable I shall be cut out by your London dutchesses and those other great ladies (my lady Hartwell, etc.) who, having disentangled themselves, one way or another, from their husbands, troop up to Oxon every year on that occasion, Dr Rowse having baited the trap for them with cold chicken and strawberries in Codrington's Library and other inducements such as our frail sex cannot resist.

On this melancholy note I must now bid you adieu, having engaged myself to go to the Infirmary this afternoon and relieve Nurse Bedpan for a while in attendance on my poor brother, of whose health, on my return, I shall not fail to advertize you and your husband; to both of whom, good sister, I commend myself.

Your loving sister,

Iris Oxoniensis

p.s. Having just returned from the Infirmary I unseal this letter to add that I find my dear brother (God be praised) vastly improved. For not only was he much cheered by sheaves of flowers sent to him in his affliction by Mercurius Cantabrigiensis from the other place (to which the news had been carried by a college cricket team), by Master

On a domestick tragedy, etc.

Lawson in London (who has mysterious channels of intelligence), and by divers admirers here in Oxon (some of whom have presumed to guess his academick name and status, but have grossly erred in it), but he hath also heard good news, which he bade me send on to you, in the matter of student stirs and Master Hart's Report thereon. For whereas Master Hart had proposed that his joint committees, wherewith he will slow down our business, should be supplied by the Student Representative Council (being their parliament, to which only a few agitators and busybodies belong), now it seems that this proposition at least must come to naught. For first, the agitators themselves, without giving themselves time to read the Report, have instantly refused to contemplate such committees, as being far below their deserts, of which they must themselves be judges; and secondly, the graduate students, being persons of sense, and seeing how the wind blows, are now openly seceding, by college after college, from that Council, as being no parliament of theirs. So now it seems that the ninnies will be left crying for the moon while the earth beneath 'em gives way and will soon swallow 'em up and so at last silence them. Which is a very comforting reflexion on which to begin the Long Vacation.

VIII

DARK AND OBNUBILATED AFFAIRS

Mercurius Oxoniensis to Mercurius Londiniensis

26 July 1969

GOOD BROTHER LONDINIENSIS

I am now (God be praised) out of the Infirmary, to which I was committed after my misadventure in Brazen-nose Lane, and glad to be back in my college, where my good scout Mudge ministers to me as well as did nurse Bedpan there, and with less disturbance of my batchelour habits; and being now permitted by the doctor to write, my first exercise is to thank all those, and you and your lady Mercuria especially, who comforted me in my distress with fruit, flowers and other tokens of sollicitude. Unhappily I cannot yet go abroad to dine, and so my news is but thin; but such as it is, I send it to you before I leave Oxon to repair my health in the house of my hospitable and true friend squire Todhunter at Quainton.

I find the face of the university in some measure changed during my absence. First, we are to have a new Chichele Professor of History, Master Southern having judged it elevation to go from that chair to preside over St John's coll., a dull place north of Balliol but monstrous rich. In his stead, after a long election, which cost in all (as I am assured) four calendar months, three sessions, and two paralytick stroaks, the electors have given us Master Barraclough, a very ingeniose man, once of Oriel coll., but since then ambulatory. 'Tis hoped he will come hither to stay, though some doubt it, his being a restless spirit. This election has been variously judged by our historians, some praising his pregnant parts, others, and especially the church-antiquaries, mumping in corners. These complain that Master Barraclough, though once one of them, has long since deserted 'em, having been struck blind, like St Paul at Damascus, *anno* 1943, by a vision of the battle fought at Stalingrad in Tartary, wherein he saw all past history wither like a scroll, and since then has had ideas above their station (philosophy, etc.): which, they say, is hereticall and not to be endured.

The other great change is the death of Dr Simpson, the Dean of Christ-church: a magnanimous man, much regretted by all, though envied in the manner of his death; for 'twas sudden and peaceful, *aetate* 77, after he had compleated his new buildings for that society and been publickly acclaimed at their great feast only four days before. He was a Canadian, born in Prince Edward Island, and had been at that House both as an undergraduate and as Hebrew Professor before being called to the deanery; in which office he quickly won the love of all, being a man of sound sense, warm heart and hospitable manners, though somewhat high in doctrine, which caused him, while he enlarged the college, to empty the cathedral. But his death, though happy for him, is very ill-timed for that coll., which now faces a hazardous succession.

For you must know that the Dean of Christ-church is both dean of the cathedral church of Oxon and head of that college, and seldom is one man fit for both parts, as things now stand, the former requiring a clergyman of the established Church, the latter a man of humane learning fit to govern a society of schollers; so that some would seek an act of Parliament to separate the two. But others oppose this as an affront to her Majesty's praerogative and the patronage of the Church, and to tradition, besides the difficulty of disentangling the property and other rights which, by now, have become so intertwined that both might suffer shock if rudely severed. Hence ingeniose spirits have proposed, as a neater remedy, that her Majesty be petitioned to revive her antient praerogative and bestow the office, undivided, upon a layman; which she could unquestionably do, without any new statute or other fuss, deaneries being benefices *sine curâ animarum*, and many worthy laymen having, in time past, served the Commonwealth therein. However, in both these courses some men sniff an objection. For they say that the fault lies not merely in the narrow qualification of the client (being a clergyman) but also in the uncertain character of the patron (or rather, of him who exercises the patronage), which could render all such pains futile, if they were but to exchange a court-chaplain for a lay courtier.

Indeed, here lies the rub. For the power of appointment to this office, whatever you may have read in *The Times* and your other silly London gazettes[1], rests not with the college at all, but with the Crown; and whereas her Majesty's Minister has customarily, in the past, consulted the college and humoured its wishes, yet he is in no way oblig'd to do so, but may stuff in, *mero arbitrio*, whomsoever he wishes to recompense or honour, as Caligula his

---

[1] The gossip-columnist of *The Times* ('PHS'), on 9 July 1969, had assumed that the Dean of Christ Church was elected by the Governing Body of the college.

Horse or our present Prime Minister his Beatles. And 'tis not to be forgot that *anno* 1965 this same Minister consulted not the Fellows of Trinity coll. (the sister foundation of Christ-church in the other place) when he imposed upon them my lord Butler as Master; which he did when he was courting the moderate men, having then but a slender majority in the Lower House of Parliament. But now the ballance is changed. Now he is secure in the Lower House and (having grown impatient of the Lords' House, and they of him) is seeking to appease rather the Root-and-Branch men who bark at his tail. Therefore (say some) 'tis not impossible but that he may use this deanery as meer politique patronage, to reward one of your fanatique parsons, such as believe in dropping bombs on our brethren in Afrique, but in little else, and some of whom ('tis thought) have long been squeaking at him for such preferment.

For the present, the Christ-church men are assuming that the Minister will follow custom and hearken to them, and so (I understand) they are now in earnest session debating whom they shall recommend; who will doubtless be one of their fellow-collegians (for those brought in from outside seldom prosper, it requiring long habituation to govern these fractious corporations): of whom Dr Henry Chadwick has been named in the Press, an eminent scholler, in every way fit for the office; but he is not alone in election, for others, apprehending a long reign, would have an older man, in whose brief term they would work to change the whole office. But they should take heed lest, in speculating on the future, they lose the present, and let the Minister insult over their division.

If the college prevail (whomsoever they prefer), the

Church will have a moderate man as Dean, and the opposite party of High-spikes, seeing this rich plum snatcht
from their mouth, will doubtless be much mortified.
However, these last are vigilant men, not to be caught
napping; and so they too have taken up arms, of the
spirituall sort. They have advertiz'd a requiem mass, with
absolutions for the repose of the late Dean's soul, and
other popish top-dressings, to be solemnized in one of
your London churches by one Dr Mascall, who describes
himself, in the publick notices, as an Honorary Student
of the House, with 'other alumni' as his acolytes: a gross
impertinency, that Dr being, *re vera*, neither an Honorary
Student nor an alumnus of the place; but these Puseyites
use not language as we do. Were I in good health, I would
go thither myself, to enjoy the comedy: for no doubt there
will be incense enough to choak 'em all, and transvestite
capers round the altar, and stuff'd pigeons let down from
the ceiling, and suchlike flim-flams. But what good all this
conjuring will do to the late Dean's soul, or to that party
in the Church (unless they can promise, by their incantations, to secure victory for the Minister in the next
generall election), I leave to your surmise.

So all roads lead back to that great states-man, whose
springs of action remain dark and obnubilated. He may
indeed, as all hope (save the Church High-spikes), con-
firm the choice of the college; but he may equally, as some
fear (who trust him not an inch), take 'em by surprise, as a
thief in the night: so that they may wake up one morning
in Margate or Portofino or Benbecula, or whithersoever
the Long Vacation has scattered 'em, to find themselves
spurned and some giddy court-parson put in to rule over
them. However, if that should happen, they have a remedy

in their hands which they will surely use, if there be any of the old spirit left in that society.

For whereas 'tis the undoubted right of the Crown to present the Dean, nevertheless that presentation carries not all with it, there being rights, powers, privileges and emoluments which the Dean enjoys by allowance of the college only and which, by a mere vote, can all be taken away and transferred to another officer whom they can elect as their Provost or President (call him what they will); and so they can, *de facto*, not only sever the college from the chapter and deprive the Dean of all his executive powers in the coll. (for he can act only mediately, through the Censors, whom he can neither appoint nor remove), but also, in effect, abridge the Crown of its power to appoint their head, reducing that succulent plum of a college headship to a dry church-prune, far less tasty in some mouths which now water for it; which would be a very proper rejoinder and may well discourage any such rash intrusion.

For the rest, the student stirs are now quite evaporated and forgot, so that in Trinity coll. (as I am told), a gyant meeting being called to discuss Master Hart's report, only two responded to the call. The only murmurs still to be heard are in a few colleges whose silly seniors, by their folly or feebleness, do invite 'em, so that we may now say, as Master Hobbes hath writ of reformation in the Church, that all these clamours do proceed from one only cause, *viz*: windy dons; amongst whose number you may rest assured that you will never find

> your loving brother to serve you,
> MERCURIUS OXONIENSIS

37

IX

FRIAR MUGGERIDGE AT AULD REEKIE

Mercurius Edinensis to Mercurius Londiniensis

13 September 1969

GUID BROTHER LONDINIENSIS

I hae received your letter of the 31st *ultimi*, in whilk you speir for news from this our Northern Athens, as it pleases you to call it; but I must send you a damping reply, for in truth we hae lang ceased to claim any sic exotick title, being weel satisfied with ourselves under our proper designation of Auld Reekie, and with our present spirituall and temporall government by the Ministers and Elders of the Kirk and the Lord Provost and Council of the City, the first founders and governors of our university. As for this Festival of the Airts, to whilk you refer as a testimony of our new enlightenment, I would hae ye know that neither we nor the guid citizens of this toun hae onything to do with sic paipish fooleries, although 'tis not to be denied that some of us may benefit privily thereby (our ministers assuring us that it is nae sin to spoil the ungodly). Indeed, had it not been for the sudden indisposition of my puir sister Euphamie, I had not been here to answer your letter, having been minded, like the best of my brethren, to let my flat and plenishings to an opulent foreigner and go, with my golf-sticks and fishing-rod, and the works of my lord Forbes and Dr Beattie, outwith the city into the kingdom of Fife; so you see that 'tis but ill-hap whilk keips me in toun at this season.

Nor does this our university offer sic news as would tickle your queasy southron palate. For we hae here neither student stirs, as in your own ill-governed School of Oeconomicks, nor disputed elections, as in that frivolous university of Oxford, whose silly Mercurius would lang syne hae been silenced by proper authority, had he opened his sawcy mouth here. But our young men mind their buiks and respect their professors, who come into their chairs without fuss, none knows how, and sit in them with dignity, expounding haillsome doctrine.

Howbeit, since you take note of the profane foreign Festival in our midst, I will tell you that although we have not yet succeeded in putting a stop to those ungodly frolicks, yet we keip up the battle and are in hopes that, in the end, by the guid sense of the clergy and citizens, we shall recover our freedom. 'Tis true, some yeirs ago certain of our bright sparks thought that they could educate and polish these rude foreigners by insinuating into their Festival some sound Scots airt, musick and letters: as Sir David Lindsay of the Mount, his merry satire against the Paip of Rome and his mistress, Dame Lechery; whilk was performed, for divers seasons, with great applause of the godly, in the Assembly Hall. And mair recently, Maister Douglas Young, a true Scotsman (who now lives maistly in Canada), put forth a witty rendering into braid Scots of a Greek play by Aristophanes, whilk I (though no lover of profane stage-plays) did out of loyalty attend on the one night for whilk it lasted. But this braw attempt to capture the Festival for our native Muses was craftily defeated by the foreigners, who are very persistent, and who contrive always to impose their own creatures as directors thereof: as now Maister Diamand, from Holland, and before that my lord Harewood, an Englishman, and others; although there were guid Scots in plenty, as my Lord Provost's own secretary, a sound orthodox man, who were willing to carry that burthen and bring things into the right frame. So now, our Scottish airts having been altogether extruded by these foreigners, and nothing now to be seen or heard but immodest English plays by W. Shakespeir and Kit Marlowe (both known paederasts) and profane or paipish Italian musick (whilk the Italians have paid hugely to bring, for we would not suffer them to come otherwise), we are now, thank God, at full liberty to attack the haill enterprise: whilk has been done weel and truly by an unlikely eneugh means, being an Englishman (but *fas est et ab hoste doceri*), *viz*: Friar Boanerges Muggeridge.

This Friar Muggeridge, as you may know, is an old rake-hell, recently turned saint, who, having been gifted with a scathing tongue, and having used it these mony yeirs to excoriate all humanity, from her Majesty downwards, has now, his other powers dwindling, consecrated this still lively member to God, and uses it with great effect against the sins, especially, of the flesh. He is not unknown in our city, for some yeirs past the foolish students of our university, haply not knowing of his conversion, elected him as their Lord Rector; in whilk office he soon showed the new spirit that had illuminated him. For first, when they cryed out for liberty to indulge those sins, he rounded upon 'em and denounced 'em all for their fleshly lusts; and then, having publickly renounced his rectorship, he clomb into the pulpit of St. Giles' Kirk, whilk was put at his disposal by its worthy minister, Dr

Whitley, and there stript and whipt it in sic style as did warm the hearts of all present; for indeed things have gone ill eneugh in this city since the good old statutes against witchcraft, adultery and trilapse in fornication were abrogated or fell into desuetude. Thereafter, like the prophet Elijah, this guid man retired for a time into the wilderness (i.e. among some shavelings in a paipish monkery in East Lothian) to open a sluice to Godward and so replenish his evacuated gall-bladder for the next devout occasion.

That opportunity has now come. For on the eve of this idolatrous Festival, the same Dr Whitley, feeling the need of a prophet to give fair fore-warning to our new Nineveh, naturally remembered the guid auld friar, and being a man zealous of the Kirk's right (and of his own: as the late Dr Warr and the Lord President of the Court of Sessions have experience[1]), he did, *motu proprio*, fetch him up from Sussex to the self-same pulpit, inviting him thence to bless, if he thought fit, the coming Festival. Whereupon our Boanerges took the hint, which was palpable eneugh, and (having seen to it that all would be fully reported: for he believes, with the philosophers, that *esse* is *percipi*) he mounted the pulpit and, stretching forth his hands, roundly cursed the haill hocus-pocus. Then, taking up his spirituall cat-o'-nine-tails, he plied it so lustily among the nine Muses (with whom he disdains any close familiarity) that 'tis much to be hoped those pagan prostitutes will never show their tattered mini-skirts and unseemly

[1] In 1962, when the Lord President of the Court of Sessions had exercised what was claimed to be his customary privilege and invited the Very Revd. C. L. Warr, Dean of the Thistle and former Minister of St Giles' Cathedral, to preach to the judges in that cathedral, Dr Whitley had disputed his right and insisted on preaching himself: which caused some stir in Scotland.

scarred bodies in this godly city again. After which, the guid friar girt up his loins and, declining all comfortable refreshment (being now a stiff Rechabite), left the doomed city, never casting a look back on it, even to reiterate his imprecations, lest he be turned to salt, or stane.

These pious labours of Dr Whitley and Friar Muggeridge have not, it must be allowed, yet banished the Festival or the foreigners from our city; but they have done much to encourage the godly, and they have been supported nobly, in particular, by one of our maist worthy city councillors, Maister Kidd, a zealous and saintly magistrate, who has sought, by laying information before the Procurator Fiscal, to have the participators in Maister Marlowe's play of King Edward II prosecuted for offences *contra naturam*; as also to have the haill Festival outlawed and the places where it has been enacted cleansed by fumigation. This proposal has not yet been carried out, by reason of the defects of our statutes; but 'tis to be hoped that when Mistress Ewing and her friends have restored our independence and national grandeur, so that we have (at least) the same freedom as they in Ulster, this *remora* shall be overcome. Meanwhile we all strive to ensure, by taking away their money and refusing to minister to their debauched cravings for new opera houses, late suppers, and suchlike carnal delights, that those foreigners who have once set foot in our city will not trouble us again.

Thus far, guid brother Londiniensis, I have cleered your errors; and now I pray you, trouble me nae mair with your letters, for, as you see, we are not here, nor wish to be, ony pairt of your dissolute Republick of Letters, ours being a city of guid order, sound doctrine and haill-

some learning: the undisturbed practick and enjoyment
whereof is the sole desire of
  your weel-affected brother to admonish and correct you,
                    Mercurius Edinensis

X

ON SAINTS & SINNERS

Mercurius Oxoniensis to Mercurius Londiniensis

22 November 1969

GOOD BROTHER LONDINIENSIS

I thank you heartily for your long letter of the 10th *inst.* Such news from your swirling estuary is always refreshing to us poor water-rats upstream. But in one matter, where you touch upon our domestick affairs, I must beg leave to correct you. For you ask when your good friend Master Prebendary John Collins, canon of Paul's Church, is to be sollemnly installed as dean of Christ-church here, so that you may honour him by your attendance on the occasion. From which I can only infer that you still persevere, *solus contra mundum*, in reading that silly London gazette *The Times*; which, having indecently exposed the poor canon (whom no one had yet named) as the likely new dean, took good care thereafter never to acknowledge its error by publishing the truth in this particular[1]. Know then that all this is meer fantasy, an *ignis fatuus* imagined by some idle speculator in the Empty Quarter of All-soules coll., or some such Desart of the Mind, who would have been better imploy'd reading Aristotle in Codrington's Library than blindly guessing about other men's affairs.

For in fact, though the publisher of *The Times* know it

---

[1] *The Times* gossip-columnist, on 13 August 1969, had suggested that the Revd. L. J. Collins was likely to be appointed Dean of Christ Church.

not, Christ-church already has a new dean, her Majesty
having long since nominated to that place our local
Chrysostom, Dr Henry Chadwick (brother of the great
Cambridge pluralist), whom the Christ-church men, *unâ
voce*, had desired as their head; and he has been duly
installed in his cathedral church, in the presence of her
Majesty's lord lieutenant, the lord bishop of Oxon,
Master Vice-chancellour, the city fathers, and the canons
and students of that college; which he has since ruled,
with universall applause of his shapely legs, graceful
manners, and golden tongue.

The ceremony of his installation was on 18th *ultimi*;
which being also the day consecrated to the blessed St
Frideswide (the patron saint of that cathedral) did supply
an occasion too good to be missed by our High-spikes,
always itching to disturb the decency of divine service
with their popish anticks. For in the midst of the sollem-
nity, they started up and must needs lead all those
grandees in a giddy procession, cavorting in and out between the church-pillars, and waving aloft an embroidered
tavern-sign of their saint; and what idolatrous genuflexions
and prostrations they enacted, writhing and unboning
their clergy limbs at the supposed ossuary of this pretious
virgin, I know not; but one who was there assures me that
he distinctly smelt a strong puff of incense; which however we may all piously hope was but an accidental fart,
released by some incontinent chorister, and mingled
perhaps with the civet and other seductive unguents with
which some of our own sex now chuse to anoint their
bodies, for what good purpose I forbear to enquire.

This St Frideswide (they tell us) was a Saxon princess
of great virtue; for besides her chastity, she mortified

45

herself strangely, sleeping on the pavement, excoriating her knees with prayer, and feeding only on barley-bread, roots and water: an example more commended than followed by the modern canons of her foundation. She came to this city *anno* 730 or thereabouts, fleeing the lust of one Algar, King of Leicestershire, who for his sin in thus pursuing a pre-contracted bride of Christ, was struck blind, on the site of the honourable and gallant captain Maxwell's Pergamon bookshop (now closed for repairs); but later, on relenting, he was cured by her intercession and no doubt turned saint or hermit too, had the monkish chronicler known how to end so edifying a story.

'Tis pity so robust and loyall a college should chuse this whining piece of she-piety for its patron, when it could have had its other neighbour St Aldate, a jolly, orthodox, old British bishop of Gloucester (a relique of his gaiters is still venerated in that cathedral), who laid about him and hewed Hengist, King of the Saxons, in pieces, and who is doubtless no less authentick than she; for although some think that the bishop is but the Old Gate canoniz'd, the lady's vouchers, when closely scrutiniz'd, are little better. I have heard the late reverend Regius Professor of Ecclesiastick History, Dr Claude Jenkins, prove, in the pulpit, and with a most melodious voice, that she too is a meer figment.

'Tis hoped by all that in this new reign we shall have fewer of these popish fooleries, for Dr Chadwick is held by all to be a man of sense and learning, and being of good birth and education, has no need to exalt himself above his lay brethren by such frills and frolicks; as also an excellent preacher, able to put together an English sentence, with subject, verb and syntax, which is rare enough in these illiterate days, and would doubtless do much good to the young, were they not artfully discouraged from hearing him.

For the rest, I have little news for you, this university being as yet, I thank God, marvellous quiet, and the new young men (except in Balliol coll.) all loyall, docile and obedient; for as yet (lacking those busy *couturiers* who each year tell the silly girls how to cut their skirts differently, to keep the dress-shops a-work) they have not discovered what the new fashion in folly shall be. Indeed, so unstable are they that I fully expect to see them taking as furiously to mortification and virginity, with St Frideswide, as heretofore, with prince Algar, to violence and fornication. For that former rage has now, as it seems, almost blown itself out, except among some silly young tutors, who, being stuck fast in their late priapean postures must needs sustain their flagging pupils at the same tension and angle of elevation, and some yet sillier seniors whom we shall doubtless find tomorrow still blindly tumbling over themselves to appease the forgotten fanatiques of yesterday.

And indeed 'tis a pretty sight to see those windy, port-soaked dons, like great overladen galleasses, still bearing onward under full spread of sail, while the nimble, lightly-trimmed undergraduates, in whose wake they had been puffing and creaking, have long since veered round and are now scudding merrily in the opposite direction. As has happened in the matter of Master Hart's great Report, of which I advertiz'd you last summer. For whereas our trembling senatours are saying portentously that this is to be the year of Hart, and pushing out long canting rigmaroles of appeasement, and whereas the

Hebdomadall Council has set up a committee to propose such measures as Master Hart has commended, putting them into like grave Wykehamicall language, behold, in University coll. (Master Hart's own college) the undergraduates have voted that they will altogether disown that Student Council which was to be built up into the centrepiece of his edifice, but which is now, thanks to the better sense of the young men, gently dissolving in ruin, unlamented by all good men and especially by

your loving brother to serve you,

MERCURIUS OXONIENSIS

p.s. Good brother, fail not to read the late Dr Swift's fifth book of *Gulliver's Travels*, which Master Hodgart has newly discovered in Dublin, and has printed in 8vo. 'Tis a pretty piece, marvellous prescient, and unquestionably authentick, describing a further visit to the Houyhnhnms and the Yahoos. Messrs Duckworth have published it, at 25s.

XI

ON ANIMAL NOISES & HUMANE SCIENCES

Mercurius Oxoniensis to Mercurius Londiniensis
6 December 1969

GOOD BROTHER LONDINIENSIS

I rejoice to learn that you have now given over reading that silly London gazette *The Times*, which can only mislead and misdirect you about our affairs, however its wearisome supplements may enlighten you upon those of Afrique or Tartary; as was clear when Master Editor, by placing Oriel coll. in Cambridge, sought to deprive our body of a learned and lively member, and then on another page, presumed to instruct us which way to vote on a domestick matter: a gross impertinency, even if (as 'tis said) that piece was writ by some new-fledged meer bachelour of All-soules coll., who by his smart answers to Warden Sparrow's *quodlibets* has got himself a place at that disastrous dinner-table. Howbeit, lest any of your friends have been misled either by that piece or by the published reports of our debates, I will now set you aright on that matter, being the proposed new course in Humane Sciences.

This term, Humane Sciences, has been borrowed (as it seems) from our old parent university of Paris, whose Faculty of Letters, having flourished for many centuries, was lately distorted into a Faculty of Letters and Humane

49

Sciences; whereupon that whole society at once went to pot, with consequences, *anno* 1968, too well known to repeat here, and too sad to insist upon[1]. This melancholy history of our dear mother should have been a salutary warning to us; but alas, we are all fated to learn by experience those calamities which we might avoid by example.

You must know then that the authour of this proposed new course in our university is one Master Pringle, a deep politician of imperious will, very persuasive and not to be gainsaid by our academick governours; who, here as elsewhere, always yield to those who press hard enough, with the appearance of numbers behind 'em, be they science professors or turbulent students. He was bred up at Winchester college (a great nursery of power), and having afterwards become Bursar of Peterhouse in Cambridge, did whack up the rents of Albany in London, which that coll. now owns, and whereon are based the rich dishes and delicate wines nightly enjoyed at that High Table. *Anno* 1961 he was elected to our chair of zoology; but before coming hither he laid down certain conditions, on which I must dilate a little; for hence spring all our woes.

His chief demand was that this university should build a great Tower or Folly in the University Parks, a delicious spot sacred to the Nymphs and Fauns, and one of the few green places still remaining to us besides that Elysian Meadow which the Christ-church men have so valiantly preserved. This tower was to be of prodigious height, dwarfing all other towers, but slender, like a gigantique

---

[1] Presumably a reference to the Paris 'Revolution' of 1968, which began in the Sorbonne.

stone beanstalk, with twenty-nine storeys, and each storey packed with animals, superimposed after their kind, as: moles in the basement, bats in the belfry, and voles, weasels, dormice, squirrels, etc. suspended between 'em. To all which Master Vice-chancellour, Master Registrar, *et al.*, being Wykehamists too, did readily assent, and a bill was duly drafted, wrapped up in grave, hieratick language, and sent down to Congregation to be passed into law.

But now (God be praised) up started the guardians of our liberties, who, having deciphered those hieroglyphs and exposed their true meaning, cried out that 'twas a cheat, contrary to our fundamentall laws, and that the Parks, being sacred, should not be so violated, even to satisfy Master Pringle or to house his animals. Whereupon Master Pringle took huff, declaring that a bargain is a bargain, that he now had Master Vice-chancellour and Master Registrar by the short hairs, and that he would in no wise let 'em go till he had his tower. So tempers waxed hot, and the debate, having begun in the Examination Schooles (archbishop Sheldon's Theatre being then closed for repairs), was afterwards removed to the publick Play-house, where the Wykehamicall oratours, by appearing on the stage in elongated masks and purple buskins, like tragick actours, could better inflame the passions of the auditours.

They began the debate by reproving us all for lack of Faith. For if we had Faith (said they) as a grain of mustard-seed, we would know that their Tower, once built, and stacked with animals, would grow mightily and pierce the boundaries of knowledge, revealing new truths for the salvation of mankind. Whereupon our academicall

Nestor, Sir Maurice Bowra, who has ruled over thirty-three generations of Wadham men, always running ahead of the youngest of them, stood up and, in a great voice, like old Simeon, cry'd out (in a rapture) that he saw a blessed vision of not one but twenty such towers, as in San Gimignano in Tuscany, multiplying our salvation. He had scarcely sat down when there was a stir at the doors, and an auxiliary army of chymists marched in, under the command of Sir Hans Krebs, at the goose-step, to vote for the Tower, so that all now thought that the day was lost; as it would have been had it not been for two stout defenders of our liberty.

The first of these was Master Blake (now Provost of the Queen's coll.), who, though a member of the Hebdomadall Council, now deserted his brethren and attacked the Tower; which he did so gallantly that a great murmur of applause arose and Sir Maurice and the Wykehamicall party gnashed their teeth furiously. After him stood up a young man who said that he too was a zoologist and knew his animals, and then suddenly he wheeled about and declared that this stuff about new truths was meer bunkum, for Master Pringle and his animals, bay they never so loud, would never overtake any new truth, their noses being all pointed in a clean contrary direction. Which bold speech, whether rightly spoken or not (for that I presume not to judge), wrought marvellously upon the auditory, so that no more speeches by the Wykehamicall party, how tragicall soever, had any effect; but when the vote was taken, 'twas found that Master Pringle's cloud-capp'd tower, and all the animals in it, had melted into air, into thin air, leaving not a rack behind.

'Twas much wondered at the time how that young man

had ventured to make that speech, our great science professors wielding such power and patronage, and making such privy treaties with one another (*manus manum lavat*), that few of their poor subjects dare dissent from them. But afterwards 'twas discovered that he had that very day been advanced to a place in Leeds, whither he was to leave that very afternoon, straightway after making his speech; and so, having purchased his liberty, he was free, at that moment, to let the cat out of the bagg.

Thus Master Pringle lost his tower; but as 'tis impossible to keep a good man down, so our worthy professor did not despair, but so wrought on our governours that in the end he was licensed to build a small hutch for his animals, in the shape of a boat, like Noah his Ark. Whereupon he set to work. But behold, when that hutch was compleat, 'twas found (like mustard-seed) to have grown strangely: not a boat but a battleship, tenfold more dreadful and deform than what had been contemplated, so that all Oxon could not find zoologists or animals enough to fill it—a million mice would be lost in a corner of it—and Master Pringle must needs find some new great monster to heave and sport in it, lest that vast empty hulk, towering over us, become a hollow joke in the university.

This new great monster is the new School of Humane Sciences which, after five years' incubation, has lately been hatch'd in our midst. It first poked its beak through the shell last August when a scientific journal (*quaere*, whence inspired?) trumpeted it abroad that this university had now boldly resolved to sweep away the old obsolete barriers betwixt one discipline and another and create a new course to end all courses; after which preamble, the monster itself clomb forth, squawking terribly in strange jargon, so that by now its whole nature is revealed. 'Tis a course for undergraduates only, who having come hither, *aetate* 18, with a smattering of school-knowledge, shall first, in three terms, frisk through the sciences of biology, geneticks, evolution, sociology, anthropology, geography, and animal noises (a science first practis'd only in the musick-halls, but now become academick), and then, in six further terms, by gadding to lectures here and there and tasting other men's courses, add seven further sciences, some theoreticall, others practicall (as, for example, 'the technology of contraception'), so that, in the end, they shall go forth as universall men, erudite *de omni scibili*, save that, by cramming all sciences into so brief a span, they shall never have had time to think of any of them.

All this being publish'd abroad, we poor college codgers were at first at a daze and knew not what to do; but soon the guardians of our liberties again bestirred themselves, and put forth a petition, signed by many hands, praying our governours to stifle this monster in its nest, while it was yet young and callow; which gave occasion, on 18th *ultimi*, to a great debate in archbishop Sheldon's Theatre, wherein the former famous debate in the Playhouse was largely resumed. For on one side Master Pringle declared that this course, like that tower, would save the world and bring in the millennium and make all things new, while on the other side 'twas urged by my lord Franks and others that this was all piffle; that our duty is not to save the world but to teach the young men to think; and that 'twill be time enough for them to chew over these subjects when they have grown teeth of

54

their own, and sharpened 'em on Aristotle, instead of being prematurely drench'd with such slopps, the swallowing whereof will turn 'em not into schollers or rationall men serviceable to the Commonwealth but into meer coffee-house oracles, fit only to puff each other's wisdom in the Sunday supplements and dazzle weak minds by smart patter on the telly.

So the battle swayed to and fro; but in the end, when the votes were counted, Master Blake being unhappily absent (at a grand feast, but this *inter nos*) and his great adversary Sir M. Bowra (though present and voting) being silent, the cause of liberty was lost by a narrow margin of 32 votes in 474; which votes, by my observation, were rather those of arts-men who wished to show themselves progressive, and to be with it, and to yield to the forward march (as they supposed) of science, than of the true scientists who, for the most part, disdained this weak and watery hodge-podge. For the medicall men, biologists, chymists, apothecaries, anthropologists etc., went out, in good order, by the same door as my lord Franks and other men of sense, but the Balliol men and the long-haired young sociologists, *et hoc genus omne*, could be seen thrusting and jostling, pell-mell, at the other door.

However, think not that the battle is yet lost. For the margin of victory being so narrow, the defeated party has exercised its right and demanded a postal vote, which is being held as I write and which closes next Monday. What shall be the issue of it none can foretell, but our busy-bodies are already astir and you can rest assured that the good old cause shall not die for lack of sustenance from
your loving brother to serve you,
Mercurius Oxoniensis

XII

THE BATTLE OF THE PHILOSOPHERS

Mercurius Oxoniensis to Mercurius Londiniensis

14 February 1970

GOOD BROTHER LONDINIENSIS

I am heartily sorry to have left your last letter so long
unanswered, but time has been hard on us all this winter.
For first my poor sister Iris, then myself (as well as my
good scout Mudge), have been afflicted with this epi-
demicall ague which has disabled so many of our friends
and has even, as I learn from the northern Mercuries,
carried off poor Edinensis. So I must beg your indul-
gence. Your solemn *quaere* about the Old-soules Club, as
you—*lapsu calami*—have called it, I have gravely con-
sidered and will fully answer in my next letter. Meanwhile, to excuse my tardiness, I shall give you a brief
survay of our Oxon affairs.

Here all remains wonderfully quiet, the student fuss
being all over and Master Hart's great report so fallen
out of fashion that only the clerks in the Registry, who
must needs compleat their game of croquet with it, and
push it through all their hoops, can still remember it.
'Tis true, some stirs are reported from Oriel coll.,
hitherto a quiet place, but lately infected (as it seems) from
Balliol, whose fanatiques, being now strangled in their
own nest, have with their dying breath spit the last dregs
of their poison across the High-street. But this short

flicker was soon snuff'd out. The fanatiques in Oriel did (as I am told) borrow enough courage from their masters to march in force into the Senior Common Room, where their governours were in session, debating the price of victuals in the beer-cellar, and, like Oliver his musque-teers, to turn 'em all out of doors; but being afterwards summoned by the Provost, and commanded to eat humble pie or risk the consequences of his wrath, their brave spirit quickly evaporated and now they have all returned quietly to their obedience.

'Tis thought that this outrage was not spontaneous by the young men, who here as elsewhere are civill enough when not misled, but instigated privily by one of their mentors, who for the past two years, by cozening some soft-headed seniors (the Provost being absent as vice-chancellour), and by divulging the *arcana imperii*, and putting glosses upon 'em, and traducing his betters, had craftily prepared it. If this be true, 'twere well to purge the place of such cockatrices, for

> *Cuncta prius tentanda, sed immedicabile vulnus*
> *Ense recidendum.*

I can tell you no more of the Oriel stirs, for that coll. is a very close place, and their feasts being frugall (and like to be attenuated by the new bursar, a strict oeconomist), I have not visited it these five years. The generall voice here in Turl-street is that the action was well fitted to the place, that society being a slow body (its embleme a tortoise), so that even its most agile and forward members, run they never so nimbly, could not leap upon the band-wagon of student power till it had stopt dead; after which there was naught to do but step off it again, and that very shamefacedly.

Of other news the chief is that the Fellows of Wadham coll. have at last elected a new Warden. Their deliberation has been strangely slow, no doubt for good reason; for this being the first such election in that coll. for thirty-two years, few of the Fellows have any experience therein, but are in that sense virgins, unfamiliar with the ins and outs of that delicious operation. Besides, 'tis a hard task for any society to replace such a head as the present patriarch of that coll., being that excellent Grecian and universall witt Sir Maurice Bowra

who, like Augustus, young
Was call'd to empire and
has governed long.

Of the process of the election I can say little, but I hear in the King's Arms (which is owned by that coll. and is the generall *locutorium* of the learned, being close to Bodley's library) that although other names have been canvassed—for there are few elections in which a chymist or a botanologer is not put forward and pressed hard by the mechanick party—the main battle has hung suspended betwixt two subtile philosophers whose affairs have long been intertwined, *viz*: Master Ayer and Master Hampshire. Of these therefore I shall now give you a brief accompt.

Master Ayer was bred up at Eaton coll., where he was very nippy at football (as Master Warden Sparrow at Winchester), and afterwards at Christ-church, where he was at first a disciple of the great professor Ryle, the Aristotle of our day for philosophy, who has writ so eloquently on Man, his mind, and Plato, his front teeth. But going then to Vienna, and there falling in with some ingeniose foreigners, he was marvellously taken by their bold doctrines and, returning to Oxon, published, *aetate* 26, a small octavo volume which so totally exploded the entire metaphysicall world that he has been hard put to it, in the last thirty years, to find anything left to philosophise about. Howsoever, being a convivial soul, and no woman-hater, he has consoled himself for these scholasticall difficulties, and having been professor both in London and in Oxon, and being of radical temper in both Church and State, he was thought fit to be head of that college. 'Tis true, some have questioned whether he, being a lover of the metropolis and its merry symposia, would be found much in the Warden's lodgings, to govern the Fellows; but those Fellows not relishing government, for themselves or the college, and the late Master Hill of Balliol (who was hanged by the young men over a year ago, as I have told you) having set the example of non-residence in his college (which has been followed by his successors, whoever they may be), that objection was set aside and a stout party set out to do battle for Master Ayer.

Master Hampshire is likewise an ingeniose philosophicall gladiator, though defter with the net than with the rapier. He was formerly of Balliol and All-soules colls.; but having been absent from Oxon these ten years, as professor first in London (where he took over Master Ayer's chair), then in the Plantations, among the high Presbyterians of Princeton, he has been much missed by his friends, who are many; for he is of agile witt, gentle temper and felicitous conversation, loved by all. He has writ prettily on Spinoza, in Master Ayer's series of books, and is no less than he (but less pungently) a friend of progress and mankind.

59

These two worthy philosophers being both named for that place, and having so much in common, 'twas difficult to disentangle 'em or decide between 'em, and how the Fellows of Wadham, in whom long disuse had bred hebetude, could have performed this delicate dichotomy, not even the barmaid at the King's Arms could tell me. But in the end, behold, the probleme is resolved, to the contentment of all. For that great states-man, our dear Prime Minister, having rewarded Master Ayer, for his philosophy, with a knighthood, he has withdrawn from the fray to savour this new dignity, and so the Fellows of Wadham coll. have served us all by fetching Master Hampshire back from the Plantations; and all good men rejoice to see the noble science of philosophy thus doubly rewarded. For 'tis not to be denied that hitherto that noble queen of science, as enthroned in Oxon, had led her most obsequious courtiers in another direction, there being more of our philosophers in Bedlam than in the books of heraldry or the seats of government. But now this reproach is wip'd away; which cannot but warm the hearts of all lovers of true learning and the Muses, and especially of

your loving brother to serve you,

MERCURIUS OXONIENSIS

P.S. Our postal vote is now counted and alas! the sons of Zeruiah have proved too hard for us. So unless we can divide 'em in the mean time, Master Pringle shall have his monstrous School of Humane Sciences. But we shall not despair. While there's death there's hope; the beast is as yet but new-spawn'd; and I doubt not but our agile mariners have harpoons in pickle even for that Leviathan.

60

XIII

ON FANATIQUES & FILES

Mercurius Oxoniensis to Mercurius Londiniensis

7 March 1970

Good brother Londiniensis

I was about to indite a long letter about the Old-soules Club but am stayed suddenly in my tracks by learning that our posts, that were once so sacred, are now everywhere profaned. For not only have some of my letters to you (which were fortunately very sober and discreet) fallen somehow into the hands of Master Lawson, who has printed them in his weekly intelligencer, the *Spectator*, but now there has broken on us this lamentable affair of Master Butterworth, his privy files, and his letter to Master Beloff; of which I shall now tell you, for it has occasioned some tumult in this peaceable university.

You must know then that this Master Beloff is a great states-man here in Oxon, being professor of government. His chair commemorates our late Prime Minister, Master Gladstone, whom Master Beloff follows in his politiques, being of the Liberal Party, like Master Jeremie Thorpe, who would rain bombs on our brethren in Afrique, and young Master Eaks, who digs up our cricket pitches at home; but Master Beloff (God be praised) is of a different mind from these and teaches the sound doctrine of law and order. He is a great oratour, whose rare wit and sharp tongue have destroyed many a proposition (and especially his own) in our Congregation House. He is also no great lover of the young, and so, on the occasion of the late stirs in the University of Warwick, he thought fit to publish, in the *Birmingham Post*, a shrewd paper urging vice-chancellours to use their coercive powers; which paper being read by Master Butterworth, the vice-chancellour of Warwick (a man of great power, who rules that university like a manufactory, and is much loved by the rich mechanicks of the place), bred an amicable correspondence between 'em.

Unhappily, the fanatiques of that university, being whipt up by their tribunes, and having insolently broken into Master Butterworth's closet, lit on this correspondence, and finding in it certain dissyllables, beyond the reach of their understanding, they at once smelt conspiracy, tyranny, popery, etc., and cry'd out that they must march in force to Oxon to smoak out this Master Beloff (who, on the first news of his discovery, had retired deep into the Old-soules Club) and burn him as an heretique, and an enemy of the people.

So they marched down from Warwick, armed with scythes, bill-hooks, etc., and on Monday last arrived in Oxon. But when they came to the Old-soules Club and saw its prodigious new fortifications (built, at huge cost, since the great siege of 1968), their spirits sank. Besides which, the club Porter (a stout guardian of the place) terrified their rustick minds by dire warnings: as, that Master Warden Sparrow had contrived strange and exquisite engines to trap and destroy them, and (even worse) that Dr Rowse was like to issue out of his window on a broomstick and bewitch 'em with his Cornish incantations.

62

On fanatiques & files

So they changed their design and went instead to Ruskin coll. (a great seminary of Liberty and Progress), where they harangued the students, curdling their blood with tales no less terrible than those they had just heard from the Porter. For they pretended that the Proctors of this university keep secret files on all of them, full of gunpowder enough, at any time, now or henceforth, to blow 'em all up; which files, they said, are all stacked, like bombards ready to be detonated, in the Clarendon Building (a stately house, built from the profits of my lord Clarendon's late loyall *History of the Rebellion* to be the university printing-house, and now used by Master Vice-chancellour and the Proctors); and thither, they said, they must all go, to capture and destroy those files, the magicall engines of tyranny, before those files should destroy them. From which speech it seems that those poor peasants thought that Ruskin coll. was part of this university, which is nowise true, and even cozened their hearers into thinking so too: so intoxicating are those words *popery* and *tyranny*.

So these two confederate armies of fanatiques, from Warwick university and from Ruskin coll., being none of them members of this university but all foreigners, bore down on the Clarendon Building, vowing that they would capture the enemy's files or die gloriously in the attempt. And indeed, by meer weight of numbers, they forced an entry; but before they could capture, as a trophy, so much as one piece of paper, they were driven off by the Watch and retired in disorder. Whereupon, the zeal of the troops cooling, their leaders thought fit to warm it up at our domestick fires, if such could be found and stoak'd; and so, next day, being Tuesday, they went to Balliol coll.

(that smouldering hearth of sedition) and by blowing on the embers, which even there were well-nigh extinct, they soon raised up a new flame; and having warmed their buttocks thereby, and become loud, confident and flatulent, they vaporiz'd again about popery and tyranny, until, by that hot air, they had puff'd out a third army, of Balliol men, with which they then set out on a second attempt to seize the Clarendon Building and its files.

Now all this stuff about files in the Clarendon Building is of course a meer *chimaera* or *ignis fatuus*. For first, as all other men know, this university has not, like Warwick, one single centre, but is rather a loose confederation of colleges, so that any register of undergraduates is kept not centrally but in their severall colleges; and secondly, even there, 'tis flattering themselves grossly to suppose that each or any of them has a file to himself, they being but *ephemera*, like may-flies or midges, whose nuisance is remembered no longer than their bite. But I fear that their present tribunes care not for truth, being more concerned to raise a tumult than to correct abuses; and now that the warre in the East Indies is abated, and Master Ho dead, and Dr Walter Adams knighted, and the price of victuals suspended in Oriel coll., and the Springboks gone home, and the cricketers from South Afrique not yet come, they can think of no more fearful bugge to frighten their doltish followers withal than this poor turnip-ghost of a great invisible File which haunts every one of 'em even unto the grave; and which is in truth no more reall than the torments of Hell, or *incubi* and *succubae*, or the conspiracy of the Elders of Zion.

Howsoever, true or false, in this sign our fanatiques were resolved to conquer, and indeed, this second time, they did take the Clarendon Building by assault. And yet, even so, their plan miscarried: for their reconnaissance having been faulty, they began by occupying the wrong room, *viz*: the Delegates' Room, which is but a Board room, seldom used, with nothing in it save one great table and some chairs and a few books of indispensable publick reference (as *Who's Who* and *Statuta Universitatis Oxoniensis* and *Raceform*) and a great portrait of her late Majesty Queen Anne of pious memory. Among which, while the fanatiques were hunting for files, the Watch closed in on them and shut 'em off from all the rest of the building.

So there was nothing they could do but entrench themselves in that room and call on their friends from the School of Technology, and from your London School of Oeconomicks, and some skin-heads from the city, as well as a few shock-heads from this university and two silly girls from Bodley's Library, to come and relieve 'em from time to time. They had some other visitors too, who came to mock 'em, and whom they were fain to throw out, but the Watch (who were with them all the time) prevented 'em: as my lady Wheare, who exasperated 'em by reading an edifying fairy tale from Muscovy. And meanwhile they kept themselves warm with rhetorique and declared on what terms they would leave the place. Which were, that Master Vice-chancellour surrender all his files to be inspected by them or their attorneys, and that hereafter they be free to read, write, amend and fabricate their own files, and that no man be free to believe anything but what they have thought fit to say in commendation of themselves, and that none of them be held responsible for anything that they do, but that they all live at ease, a law unto themselves, doing what they will, as in the abbey of Thelema, maintained at the charge and by the labour of our honest citizens; and until this treaty should be signed, they said, they would not leave the Delegates' Room.

Which terms Master Vice-chancellour and the Proctors having repudiated with contempt, and refusing altogether to parley with such mangy cattle, as cloven in mind as in hoof, they remained in their pound until Monday, when, being as weary of treading in their own dung as we of their lowing and braying, they shambled forth in a lame, disorderly fashion; and now such as may be found to belong to this place will be rounded up and sorted out and sent to the byre or (as is hoped by many) to the butcher.

'Tis asked by some why Master Vice-chancellour did not cause these creatures to be driven out sooner rather than let 'em sit there for six days defiling the place; but the law, it seems, is mighty defective in this matter, since the great business of Master Wilkes and the judgment on generall warrants, *anno* 1765, as was shown lately when a parcel of greasy hippies invaded certain premises in your bowling-alley of Piccadilly. Howsoever, we hope to see all that changed; and whichever party in the state shall change it, so that we have no more of these taedious intrusions, may rely on the blessing and support of
your loving brother to serve you,
MERCURIUS OXONIENSIS

p.s.: I shall send my letter on the Old-soules Club, being very delicate, by a new way, to elude Master Lawson's nippy fingers; for I would not have it published, lest Master Warden Sparrow see it and find means to entangle me in his long robe.

XIV

ON A PROFESSOR & A NOVELLIST

Mercurius Oxoniensis to Mercurius Londiniensis

21 March 1970

Good brother Londiniensis

The news that you send me, *viz*: that your silly London gazette *The Times* has publickly declared me to be none other than our worthy Regius Professor of History[1], has diverted us in Oxon no less hugely than you in London, all men recognising at once both the impossibility and the absurdity of it. Which whether it were done to exasperate him or me, or to breed trouble betwixt us, I can assure you that it has signally failed; for that professor and I, chancing to meet of late at the ordinary, forgot our mutuall differences (which have been sharp enough, he having much resented my late tart observations upon him[2]) and made merry together over this exquisite new piece of folly.

You ask me how it could come about that Master Rees-Mogg, the editor of that gazette, who is otherwise a prudent and scholler-like man, could publish so egregious an error. My answer is that assuredly 'twas a trick played upon him by one Master Auberon Waugh, a scurrile scribbler who was until lately employed by Master Lawson

---

[1] This error was committed by *The Times* gossip-columnist 'PHS' on 9 March 1970.

[2] Presumably a reference to letter IV above.

of the *Spectator*; but having been very properly dismissed by him for gross impertinency (which decency forbids me to particularise), he has now found service under Master Rees-Mogg and is neglecting no occasion to take his revenge upon his late patron. He has even sought means to cut him out in his own fief; for Master Lawson being ambitious to serve the Commonwealth in parliament as burgess for the borough of Slough (a romancy seat: see Sir J. Betjeman's delicate poeme thereon), this Master Waugh, though of the same party in the state, is now busily writing against him, and even threatening to promote a candidate to challenge him at the poll—not in hopes to win over the major part of the electors (which were impossible), but solely to seduce some of the sillier of them and so to open a way to their common adversary Mistress Lestor; which shows to what lengths the spirit of revenge will carry a man, if he be not well grounded in the principles of true religion.

Moreover, 'tis not to be forgot that this Master Waugh may pretend grounds for seeking revenge not only upon Master Lawson, as his former patron who has discarded him, but also upon the Regius Professor himself, as an hereditary enemy of his house. For you must know that this Master Auberon Waugh is the son of that ingeniose novellist and incomparable witt, the late Master Evelyn Waugh, betwixt whom and our professor there was some difference, of long standing: which difference was bred originally, as it seems, by discrepancy of religion, though afterwards quicken'd by publick controversy; for as the novellist used to mix much gall in his ink, so the historian could ply, at times, a sharp-pointed quill. Of this ancient difference I will now advertize you, so that this whole new affair may be cleerly understood.

You must know then, first of all, that whereas our worthy professor (though of an antient recusant family, but long since reclaimed) has always been a sound protestant and a loyall member of the true Church established by law amongst us, that late novellist moved in a clean contrary direction: for although bred up in the same true Church, he was afterwards perverted from its wholesome doctrines and became a papist—and that of so precise and zealous a kind that successive popes and all their cardinalls must pant hard to keep up with him in the nicer points of observance; after which perversion his rare witt became incrassated and the sparkle of his novels was sadly dimm'd.

The evangelist who performed this favour for him and received him into that church was none other than that dexterous angler for soules, Fr Martin D'Arcy *e soc. Jesu* (happily still with us), who, being then Master of Campion Hall, a Jesuit seminary in Oxon, did by his gawdy lures and epicurean baits (for he was marvellous hospitable) land, and serve up to his master the Pope, one or two noble gudgeon (*quaere* whether my lord Longford not one of them?), although some other stout fish brake his line and got away: as, *e.g.*, my lord . . . (but such names are not for paper).

Now our novellist, being thus firmly hook'd, did afterwards resolve, as a grateful proselyte, to offer to his ghostly confessor the first-fruit of his newly sanctified labours. He therefore dash'd off a panegyricall accompt of the eponymous hero of that seminary, *viz*: Master Edmund Campion: a simple Jesuit who, with a more subtile companion, one Master Persons, came over from beyond seas, *anno* 1580 or thereabouts, to seduce Her Majesty's subjects from their allegiance; but being sniff'd out and caught, he afterwards suffered the extream penalties of treason. Which book, though insipid enough to the taste of us protestants, and sadly lacking in historicall substance and exactitude (see the excellent witty notice of it by the late Mistress Rose Macaulay in Master Connolly's late broadsheet *Horizon*[1]), nevertheless, being prettily trick'd out for its purpose and laid at Master D'Arcy's feet, was at once pick'd up by the papists (or at least by such of them as hang around the Jesuit church of Farm-street in Mayfair) and, being by them cry'd up as a work of rare genius, *etc., etc.*, bred many imitations; so that by now there is scarce one of those forty martyrs (as we must now call 'em) but has his *encomium*, and the present bishop of Rome, to satisfy those Jesuits (who push very hard), as well as to divert attention from his own domestick difficulties (celibacy, the pill, *etc., etc.*), is fain to canonise the whole caboodle of 'em.

Howbeit, our grave Regius Professor, being of a different mind, did not join in this devout chorus of popish flibbertigibbets. On the contrary, he was so rash as to touch lightly (but in another sense) on the same matter; which he did more than once, somewhat pungently, and especially in an essay entituled 'Twice Martyr'd', which he has since reprinted in his volume of *Historicall Essays*, publish'd *anno* 1957; whereby he incurred the wrath of all those Mayfair papists, so that they made waxen

---

[1] 'The Best and the Worst: Evelyn Waugh', in *Horizon* No. 84, December 1946.

images of him, and stuck pins into them, uttering fierce incantations, and cry'd out against him at their symposiack meetings, threatening to put rat-poyson in his port-wine, *etc.*, and would have had him removed altogether out of Oxon (had their conjuring any effect) as a corrupter of the young and a danger to faith and moralls. This controversy continued merrily for some years and, both parties being egg'd on by their friends, caused much diversion to the profane.

Now 'tis easy to suppose that this young sprig Master Auberon Waugh, having been bred up at that time and in that family, and being (as we must suppose) a young man of exemplary piety, both in his religion (however defective) and towards his late parent, has sucked in some of the warm air thus engender'd; of which, by now, he must naturally wish to ease himself by evacuation. And this, together with his animosity against poor Master Lawson, I verily believe to be the whole cause of this praeposterous error into which Master Rees-Mogg (a trusting soul) has allowed himself to fall in publickly confounding together two such opposites as myself and the Regius Professor; which confusion can only cast yet further discredit on his gazette and pay him back for his imprudence in recruiting for it such a *boutefeu* as this Master Auberon Waugh. But as such an error by him can never mislead any rationall man, I will say no more of it, but subscribe myself

your loving brother to serve you,

Mercurius Oxoniensis

XV

ON STUDENT STRIKES & PASQUILLS

Mercurius Oxoniensis to Mercurius Londiniensis

25 April 1970

GOOD BROTHER LONDINIENSIS

I am glad to learn, from your letter of the 8th *inst.*, that those absurd speculations of Master PHS, in *The Times* gazette, confidently declaring me to be none other than my old adversary (now reconcil'd), the Regius Professor of History, have occasion'd only mirth and ridicule among our friends in the metropolis. Not that I ever doubted the good sense of most of you there; but there are always some innocent souls who will believe anything, in our academick world no less than in Printing House Square. Yet I must confess that in these last days I have sometimes wished that the doctrine of Master PHS, how praeposterous soever, had been believed, in order to draw off from me some imminent dangers.

For after all this ruffianly sword-play and aërial piracy by the student fanatiques in Japan, and this barbarous kid-napping and then murther of that poor ambassadour in Guatemala[1], the timidity of my nature begins to assert itself. I can brave it out with the best in a college meeting

---

[1] In April 1970 Japanese student revolutionaries, armed with swords, hijacked an air-liner and forced the pilot to fly it to North Korea. About the same time revolutionaries in Guatemala kidnapped the German ambassador, Count Karl von Spreti, held him hostage for their demands, and finally shot him.

72

or Congregation, and stand resolute for the cause, *Athanasius contra mundum*, in committee, or in caucus, or at dessert. But I like not cold steel nor hard shot; and if such tricks are to be played on us here (*quod Deus avortat*), though I wish no ill to that worthy professor, better on him than on me, say I. He has a stout constitution and can give blow for blow, but my poor body is craz'd with age and bent with study. I relish not the thought of being whisk'd off to the Antipodes in a captive flying-machine by fanaticall gladiatours from Balliol coll., nor of being shot through the head in some bramble-thicket in Hell Copse or Badgers' Bottom (whence squire Todhunter flushes his foxes) by masked and bearded desperadoes from Oriel coll. For these are the two colls. in which our fanatiques can still be heard spluttering. Of my own comfortable coll. in Turl-street I have no such fears, the young men there being all of exemplary conduct.

Alarm'd by these *Mormo's* or hobgoblin fears, I had almost thought of taking flight. Come, said I, 'tis time for a sabbatique term of absence from Oxon; and why should I not, at my age, go a-cruising with my dear sister Iris in the South Seas and there refresh my mind in some abstruse by-ways of sound learning? But this my design, how tentative soever, was no sooner whisper'd abroad than I was besieged on all sides by flattering dehortations. For first, the most prudent of my fellow-collegians begged me to desist from any such project, saying that 'twas absolutely necessary that I remain here at my post, not only to teach the young men the right interpretation of Aristotle his *Politicks*, but also to utter sound doctrine in our college senate, where (said they) 'tis much needed, to stiffen the gellies; and secondly, an ambassage of my pupils, coming to my door, in a very respectfull manner, offered themselves as a body-guard (as that famous Association for the late Queen Elizabeth, of glorious memory) to defend my life against kid-nappers or assassins, or, at the worst, to avenge my death at such hands; whom I heartily thanked and refreshed with some choice Rhenish wine sent to me by Master Lawson and other gratefull readers of these my letters.

Finally, to resolve my last doubts, there has come into my hands a curious paper. 'Tis a pasquill put forth after the dismall failure of their anticks at the end of last term, by a junto of fanatiques who call themselves (observe well their jargon) 'a meaningful organisation of militant students at Oxon to fight the power of the authorities'; and it has been sent to me by a good friend who collects such *trivia* for his album or file (though we use not that word now, as ill-omen'd) to give mirth to his little grandchildren. This pasquill called upon all students throughout the land, in revenge for the spanking they of Oxon had received from Master Vice-chancellour and the Proctors, to cease parleying with vice-chancellours etc., as a pack of obstinate disobedient currs, and instead to bring 'em sharply to heel by calling 'A NATIONALL STUDENT STRIKE'; which last words they have writ thus, in black letters, such a strike being, as they say, an absolute necessity if they are to stave off final defeat and, thereafter, an eternall dark-night of tyranny, slavery, etc.

A nationall student strike . . . O noble prospect! O blessed freedom for us poor college mokes, tied fast to the treadmill of lectures, tutorials, examinations! O liberty, sweet liberty! Why then (said I) should I sollicit a sabbatique term, at some cost to myself? For besides disappointing my friends, I must spend my accumulated credit in that sort, and shift my pupills to other extemporary tutours, and even entrust the care of the college cellar, which I have managed these thirty years, to some untried deputy. Here is a sabbatique term freely offer'd to all of us! The wicked shall cease from troubling us and we shall be at rest in our colleges, every man under his vine and under his fig-tree, reading our books and drinking our port-wine like gentlemen once again. And those poor blind creatures, for wilfully deserting their studies, shall be docked of the subsidies which the publick pays 'em for that purpose, and which they so grossly abuse, and shall be obliged to earn their bread by turning spits or carting dung or skinning whales, or other such honest employments, far more necessary to the commonwealth than reading profane and seditious works of sociology.

So I have given over my plans of travel, and now, instead of idle discourses from Trincomalee or Otaheite, you shall continue to receive my pregnant letters of news from Oxon; which news I shall now compleat, by telling you somewhat more about this pasquill which I have received, and the circumstances in which it was writ. To which end I must take you back to my late letter, concerning the fanatiques who shut themselves up, and were besieged, for the space of a week, in the Clarendon Building.

Know then that when those fanatiques left that building, on Monday 2nd March, pretending thereby to have won some notable victory over the powers of darkness, they straightway called all men to gather in the Union, or mock-parliament of the university, for a great assembly, to register and compleat their triumph; which assembly was presided over by one of your practis'd agitators from London, who whipt and stript it in their usual fashion. At this great meeting, six apostles were chosen, all known fanatiques (some of Balliol coll., some formerly of Warwick university or Ruskin coll.), who were charged straightway to go and threaten Master Vice-chancellour, in the name of them all; which they did, in an insolent paper (since fallen into my hands) requiring compliance with all their demands within two days: failing which they would do great things.

But these threats being totally ignored, and no great things happening, these poor agitators soon fell into contempt; from which they sought to extricate themselves by calling ever more meetings, and shouting ever louder, to an ever dwindling auditory; until, on Thursday 12th March (being the time for sentence to be pronounced on their ringleaders), they gathered round the Proctors' office crying out, as in a trance, 'Kill the pigs! Kill the proctors!' and suchlike indecencies, very painfull to loyall ears; after which they broke into Bodley's quadrangle, in a tumultuary fashion, and would have broken into his Library too, had not the great gate been closed against 'em; so they pranced around chanting 'Kill the proctors!', till they were weary, and then went away. All which gained them nothing (the proctors being men of stout heart and good sense), nor saved their leaders from due punishment.

So at last, that evening, in their despair, they called a meeting at Somerville coll. (a female seminary, once of high repute); and 'twas here that they blew their trumpet-call for a generall student strike, as their last remedy, being already *in extremis*. At the same meeting they propounded also the setting up of a Committee of Defence, to sit in Oxon throughout the vacation, countering the machinations of their enemies (who have better things to do than machinate against such poor buzz-flies) and to ensure (again you will mark their jargon) 'a permanent base for further militant action'; which base, how permanent it will be, resting on such froth and bubble, I leave to your imagination.

Our next term being now about to begin, we shall soon know whether the call to the generall strike has been issued and obeyed. Meanwhile I do but observe that the style and substance of their papers sufficiently show (besides their illiteracy) how sensible these poor fanatiques are become of the contempt and ridicule into which they have brought themselves. 'Tis now to be hoped they will turn on their leaders, who have caused them thus to expose their upturn'd bare buttocks (which nevertheless are the seemliest parts of some of them) to Master Bullock's birch-rod; and in particular, on that practis'd agitator of yours, whom I beg you henceforth to keep at home, and not send hither to trouble

your loving brother to serve you,

MERCURIUS OXONIENSIS

p.s. I have today sent to you, by a most secret new way (for it must on no account fall into Master Lawson's hands), a long letter on the Old-soules club. Pray acknowledge receipt thereof: I shall not rest till I know it safe in your hands.

XVI

HOW THE GREAT DEBATE BEGAN

Mercurius Oxoniensis to Mercurius Londiniensis

16 May 1970

Good brother Londiniensis

I am much disquieted to learn that my long letter on the Old-soules club has come to your hands so slowly. I would accuse no man rashly, but at this time (as we know from daily examples), even the most confidentiall papers may go astray. Pray examine the seals: are they still inviolate? If that letter has miscarried, I do protest that our correspondence will cease. But I trust that no such disaster has befallen us, for our news already is bad enough.

First, our hopes of a nationall student strike, which had risen so high, are now quite dash'd. The new term has begun, and not an undergraduate is missing. 'Tis true, a few days before term, in an attempt to save the last reliques of their credit with their followers, our chief fanatiques went up to your city, saying that they would seize the citadel of the Nationall Union of Students and thence proclaim their generall strike. But they failed dismally; for the leader of that Union, one Jack Straw (a sturdy peasant), being roused suddenly from his pallet, hastily fetch'd up his coadjutor Wat Tyler and other allies and beat off those poor cod's-heads, who limped back hither, with bloody noses and bruised buttocks, to be a

How the great debate began

laughing-stock to their own silly myrmidons[1]. So that now we can say that civill warre has indeed broke out amongst 'em, as we had hoped; which is some consolation for all that we must now suffer, both by their presence and by a second burden which we are to carry this term.

For now at last our Congregation, or legislature, is to debate, clause by clause, that great Report (about which I have already writ to you) of Master Verulamius Hart. 'Tis now a full year since Master Hart laid this Report at the feet of Master Vice-chancellour, who had set him a-work; and throughout this last year our Hebdomadall Council, with the Clerks of the Registry, have been transforming it (sometimes amended) into draft statutes for our deliberation; which draft statutes having been publish'd at the close of our last term, 'tis now our part to consider whether we will vote upon 'em, as presented to us, or have them amended. So, all through this last vacation, our publick-spirited brethren have caballed together in common-rooms and coffee-houses, and now, throughout this term, Tuesday after Tuesday, we poor college snails must uncoil and disnestle ourselves from under our comfortable old stones, and creep to the Congregation-house to debate the twenty-nine ingeniose amendments which from all sides have been propounded.

This great debate began last Tuesday 8th May; which day had scarce dawned before the trumpeters on both sides sounded the call to battle. For first, our worthy legislators, while still somnolent and but slowly uncurling over their breakfast muffins, were startled to learn from Master Beloff (the coryphaeus of the Liberal Party

[1] This attempt to capture the headquarters of the N.U.S. in London was made, and repelled, on 22 April 1970.

among us, who blows his top from time to time in your London *Times*) that all our universities are being led by their vice-chancellours into a new Dark Age, and that if we stand not firm against Master Hart and suchlike innovators, we must expect barbarian inundations, the extinction of letters, and a thousand years of monkery and popery, chaos and old Night. Then, on venturing out of doors, our blood was further chilled by chalk-scribbles in all the streets calling on the fanatiques to gather with their tom-toms and tomahawks at Captain Maxwell's late bookshop and thence march boldly upon archbishop Sheldon's theatre (where Congregation was to meet) and see justice done to their demands. And indeed, in the afternoon, when we assembled there, we did find a few scruffy creatures lounging at the outer gates of that theatre, with a placard which none heeded, for it was held the wrong way.

Within the theatre, the first to speak were those who wished to return to the golden age when Saturn was king and all men behaved civilly without the need of laws. Their oratour was Master Lucas, a philosopher (but of Merton coll.: not one of our chop-logicians). He holds, with his praedecessors in that coll., that the present state of things is always right and good, provided that it does not diverge from the previous state, which would not have existed had it not been approved by God: a very sound doctrine which, being generally accepted in Merton coll., has contributed to the undisturbed peace of that place. However, for all his rare eloquence, he won but few votes, the major part of the assembly holding that those golden days had gone, alas, for ever.

After this rose the friends of liberty and progress (so-call'd). These would put all discipline in the hands of undergraduate tub-preachers, who should make and change the rules without any statutes save one to secure them that liberty, or any penalties except by their leave: so that they could come naked to lectures, or drop turds in Master Vice-chancellour's throne, or copulate *contra naturam* in their college chapels. This party was supported by a canting fanatique from St John's coll. (formerly of Ruskin coll.), who stood up wearing no coat (but a Phrygian cap) and told us that we must not consider what was just or rationall, but yield what he and his friends demanded, which was all power to the people, i.e. themselves; which speech was applauded loudly by a parcel of undergraduates in the gallery (who should have kept silence) but by none whatsoever in the chamber. This party (God be prais'd) was soundly thrashed; for when the poll was taken, they had no more than 21 votes against 232, and those only from long-haired sociologists, Balliol men, etc., whose votes should not have been allowed, had the good old order been kept: for coming into the chamber in bare feet or sandals and without coats or neck-ties, they should have been thrust out by the bedells instead of being suffered to shamble out through the Ayes' gate and there be counted.

Others also put forth other amendments, among whom Master Hart himself persuaded us to remove a clause making incitement to disorder itself penall: which he held to be too imprecise and so dangerous to liberty. Truly I am almost in love with his Socratique rationality: for he asks not how far we should yield, or where resist, but proceeds always by cleer reason from generall truths. But some fear that he errs in presuming all men to be as rationall as he. They say that 'tis a mistake to exchange traditionary authority for novel paper constitutions, how perfect soever, when there are fanatiques abroad who might have been controuled by the one but will soon find means to evade or exenterate the other. Those who will not suffer her Majesty's Secretary of State to expound his reasons in their Union[1] will hardly listen to those of Master Hart in the mouth of a Proctor; and 'tis not to be forgot how the pupills of Socrates himself did acquit themselves in the politiques.

Thus the victory, at all times, went to the moderate men who would apply Master Hart's doctrines. But 'tis too soon to conclude, for there are twenty-five other amendments still to be debated, and many profound and witty speeches still to be made: as, *e.g.* on student participation by Master Warden Sparrow, who, being happily unencumber'd by undergraduates in his own college, has no wish to meet 'em on committees, at least until there be a statute obliging 'em to wash and shave; which Master Hart has omitted to supply. Besides, who knows how punctually our legislators will attend these continuing debates, on summer afternoons, when they might be reading novells in their college gardens or watching cricket-games in the Parks? 'Tis to be hoped that all our brethren will prefer their duty to their pleasure, lest by a surprise vote, in a thin house, we suddenly find ourselves in Master Beloff's Dark Age, or the millennium of the fanatiques.

To compleat our sorrows we have suffer'd, this last

---

[1] H.M. Secretary of State for Foreign Affairs, Mr Michael Stewart, came to address the Oxford Union on the policy of the Labour government towards the U.S. invasion of Cambodia. Radical students prevented him from speaking.

se'nnight, some grievous losses. Of Mistress Starkie I have writ before: she was an originall, whom all men loved for her warm heart, conviviall ways, and colour'd clothes. She dress'd herself as a French sailor, out of love for that nation and its letters, which she taught in Somerville coll., leading those tender virgins through the works of Messieurs Baudelaire, Verlaine, Rimbaud, Gide, etc.: which must have enlarg'd their vocabulary, if not their experience; but these are yielding times. Of Sir John Beazley, the incomparable pot-critick, I need not tell you: among Grecians he is already *fama super aethera notus*. He was of a ripe age, 84, and had survived his lady, a notable character. She was of Smyrna, and wore a turban of many colours. At one time they contriv'd to live in Christchurch, in a canonry (*quaere*, how managed?), with their domestick goose as a companion, which they cherished mightily, and put to graze in the Great Quadrangle. 'Twas to this same bird (which pre-deceased 'em) that Master Harold Acton, our Florentine virtuoso, then an undergraduate, showed such memorable civility. (He had stumbled over it in the twilight, returning, in a grey top hat, from the horse-races at Ascot.) My lady Beazley never forgot that courtesy[1]. 'Tis unlikely that any of our modern undergraduates, even of that coll., would show such deference, at least to a reall goose.

Finally, we are now to lose another worthy colleague. For Master Professor Gallagher, our learned historian of

---

[1] It seems that on this occasion Mr Acton (who is noted for his exquisite manners) picked himself up, dusted his trousers, and then gravely bowed to the goose, doffing his top-hat and expressing his apologies for the involuntary collision. Lady Beazley, who observed the episode from her window, and who had expected a very different response, was enchanted by his civility and became a warm friend of Mr Acton in consequence.

the Plantations, is shortly fleeing to Cambridge. 'Tis a sad blow to us, perhaps irreparable; but his chair here is annex'd to Balliol coll., from which the flight of good men is now generall. As you say, that coll. is past hope of recovery till it have a Master again. I hear that the late Dr Hill is now much regretted: fresh flowers set daily on his grave, etc. 'Twas precipitate of the young men to string him up, besides being an ill precedent, which I hope will never be repeated either on your person or on that of

your loving brother to serve you,

Mercurius Oxoniensis

XVII

THE OLD-SOULES CLUB

Mercurius Oxoniensis to Mercurius Londiniensis

30 May 1970

Good brother Londiniensis

I am heartily glad that my unvarnish'd accompts of our daily life in Oxon have so put you in love with this place that you would willingly exchange your metropolitan distractions for our singular pursuit of learning. But when you add that, for that purpose, you would, on my recommendation, seek admittance to our famous Old-soules Club, then I must confess that I admire rather your courage than your prudence; for 'tis cleer you know not the intricacy and the hazards of that mouldering labyrinth, nor the craft and vigilance of the great Minotaur whom you must first tame if you would penetrate it. However, at this your entreaty, I shall be your friend, and, like Ariadne, shall give you a clew of strong packthread to guide you by, spun out of my own long observation and curious survay of that place.

Know then that this famous club was formerly a college, called All-soules college (in the French tongue, *collège des morts*), being founded by the late archbishop Chichele, in order that the members thereof might pray for the soules of those who died fighting our neighbours the French at Azincourt, *anno* 1415; which soules were then thought to be still in Purgatory. But Purgatory being since abolish'd by act of Parliament, this function has ceased. At one time there were some few undergraduates in the place, as singing-boys; but the Fellows finding 'em either too many or too few for their purposes, they too have ceased; as also have those Fellows who were formerly admitted as Founder's kin, and who would from time to time drop in to soak up the college port and enjoy a hand of *ombre* or *picquet*; so that the club is now limited to its proper Fellows, who are very jealous of any new members, as likely to eat up their endowments (though huge) and to disturb their sweet *otiums*.

For indeed 'tis a delicious place, as they take care to rub into those of us who have not the felicity to be among 'em; for they have seen fit to set up, conspicuously, in a vestibule through which their guests must pass, an inscription, of doubtful latinity but cleer import, *viz*:

> *Frustra alii strepitum cupiant evadere mundi;*
> *Hic sociis remanet Chicheliana quies;*

which one has english'd thus:

> From the world's din you vainly seek release;
> We Fellows of Old-soules alone have peace.

This smug distich was writ, as I understand, by the late Sir Dugald Malcolm, an ingeniose Scotchman who, having become monstrous rich by his prudent traffick with the poor kaffirs of South Afrique, was able thereafter to return to this club and indulge his Muses. From this you may judge how closely those Fellows guard themselves against new intruders, for whom there are now but three ordinary ways of entry; and the gates of all three are strictly controuled by the Warden and his Manciple, who like not to see new faces.

The first way of entry is by examination; but this way is not suitable for you, being open only to young batchelours, such as have lately pleased their publick examiners by their smart answers in the Schooles. These, being afterwards further refin'd by a second and private examination, set and judged by the Fellows of the club, are then invited thither to dine, and scrutiniz'd closely, and finally, if thought ingeniose and docile enough, and of civill manners (which is not to be despis'd in these days), admitted to membership. After which, having once tasted the lotus-fruit of that enchanted island in our boysterous seas of Academe, their course is set. For unless, like Ulysses, they get away quick (as severall have wisely done), they trouble themselves no more with learning, but either dissolve into pop-singers, gossip-scribblers, Grubstreet news-mongers, coffee-house oracles, etc., or disappear altogether from the known world and are never seen or heard again.

'Tis true, in the last thirty years, there have been two or three Fellows of this sort who, by stedfastly refusing the lotus-fruit, how tempting soever, have nobly served the Commonwealth of Learning, and whose names you will hear brought forth on occasion. But be not deceiv'd; for these are but the honest oxen in a travelling circus, who snort and heave to pull the richly painted cart wherein the pantaloons and performing sea-lions and antick marmosets do idly frisk and gambol.

However, 'tis not to be denied that these young Fellows

by Examination may also, in due course, serve their turn. For certain of them, carefully sifted, are, after the expiry of their first fellowships, kept on (as Ethiopians, at a low diet) under the new title of 'Fifty Pounders'; who, coming to the feasts and meetings of the club, do act—together with certain seniors call'd 'Distinguished Fellows' (being ambassadours, judges, archbishops, etc., elected *ad hoc munus*)—as Master Warden's Janizaries or *corps d'élite*, always ready, at time of need, to be wheel'd into action, in order, by their votes (which in the most vitall affairs are secret and unaccomptable), to frustrate the creation of new fellowships (even if advertiz'd), or the election of new Fellows, or the granting of rooms to new professors, or the building of new rooms in Master Warden's garden, or any other unseasonable change. For Master Warden loves not change, holding all change (unless backward, as cobbling the High Street, or abolishing motor-cars, or reviving antient sinecures) to be but another stage in the fall of man and the loss of our innocency.

For this cause, Master Warden greatly mislikes the second way of entry into the club, over which he has less controul. This is the way *ex officio*, by election to certain dignities in the university which by statute are annexed to that club, as the Regius Chair of Civill Law or the Chichele Chairs of History, Internationall Law, History of Warre, Oeconomick History, *etc.*; whereby (although in most such elections the club has two votes, which is a great safe-guard) 'tis possible that some dangerous Serpent may slide into that Paradise. However, these professors being of a ripe age, and having their other avocations, and there being no undergraduates to draw 'em together and fix 'em in the place, they have hitherto

88

been docile enough; besides that many of 'em reside generally abroad, as the Regius Professor of Civill Law, who resides chiefly in Northern California (with occasional excursions to Constance in Switz); and if new professors should insist on coming to Oxon, they are likely to hear that there are no rooms for them in the club, or a garret only, the best rooms being kept empty for those senior Fellows who live abroad, as Dr Rowse, who for the last ten years has resided chiefly in Southern California, using the Old-soules Club as a summer cottage when that climate becomes too hott for him.

'Tis true, this good doctor has this year broke his habit and granted us his presence in Oxon even in winter; for which welcome innovation we know not, as yet, the reason. Some suppose that he is cooking up a great stinking bombard wherewith to blow-up, sky-high, those impertinent criticks who dissent from his judgment of certain plays and sugar'd sonnets of Master William Shake-speare, his familiar friend. Others believe that the affable red-skins of California (a gentle tribe, not cannibal) have invited him to enjoy a vacation here, on full pay, so that he in Oxon (being a place of more competition) may rest his voice, and they in California their ears. Others again think that Master Warden himself has entreated him to stay, to help him keep down the baser sort and preserve the club from innovation. Which of these reasons (if any) is true, I know not; but by me any reason will be accompted good which keeps for us that incomparable doctor.

The third and last way into this delicious club is by means of Visiting Fellowships. This is a new device, and therefore misliked by those that love not innovation but judged necessary as a prophylactick, to preserve that antient body from finall decomposition. For you must know that some years past, when our politick physician, my lord Franks, was called in to examine all our organs[1], he open'd the very entrails of that plump body, and tweak'd 'em somewhat painfully with his forceps, saying that 'twas cleer too much had been spent on epicurean dinners, and too little on the Muses, and hinting darkly that so plethorick a body could not hope to live; which severe observations were afterwards carried further by a renegade Fellow, one Master Caute, who took it upon himself to anatomize that whole society, not privily, as I do to you, but publickly, in Master Lasky's gazette *Encounter*, with a sharp, polish'd, and (some said) poison'd lancet[2]. Whereat Master Warden and the Fellows, in a panique, cast around for palliative plaisters and cataplasms, crying out that they would mend their ways and give all they had to the poor, so they might be suffered to live and not die, nor either fling open the gates of the club to new members or alter the delicate ballance of votes within it: which would be but a slower form of death.

So, after laying out some thousands of pounds upon certain deserving (and powerful) bodies within the university, and encouraging my lady Hartwell and other great persons, to protest, in their gazettes and gossip-columns, that my lord Franks's observations were unjust and that

[1] See *University of Oxford: Report of Commission of Enquiry. Volume I—report recommendations and statutory appendix; volume II—statistical appendix*. (Commonly called the Franks's report and published by the OUP on May 12th 1966.)
[2] *Encounter*, March 1966.

the club was a mighty force for good in the university (i.e. invited 'em to its grand feasts), they hit on this pretty engine of Visiting Fellows, to whom they offer bed and board (but no votes) for a term or a year, so that they may read in Bodley's Library and hob-nob with the natives. Which device I cannot commend too much, both as a preservative of that antient club (its prime purpose) and also for the reall, if incidentall benefits which it has brought to us; for thereby we have had among us many worthy men from other universities, both here and beyond seas. But whether you, good brother, could squeeze through that new gate, even with such commendations as I could give you (which might be warmer in my mouth than in Master Warden's ears) is a question not easily to be resolved.

Nevertheless, 'tis by this gate or none that you must creep in. Therefore my counsell to you is that you lose no time in paying court to Master Warden. He is the great states-man who alone, by his ingeniose managery, his skilfull procrastination, his secret reserves of votes, and his influence in high places (as the Beefsteak Club, Roxburghe Club, etc.), can rule that society. 'Tis true, not all the Fellows follow him willingly through all his *ambages*, which are infinitely subtile, so that few have leisure to unravel 'em; but when Hannibal is *ad portas*, all men turn to a Fabius Cunctator, and ever since my lord Franks, with his elephants, crossed the Cornmarket, the senatours of the Old-soules Club have cluster'd round their Warden, who alone, as they now admit, *cunctando restituit rem*.

Nor is this his only service to that society. For having first saved it from the diabolicall two-pronged fork of my

lord Franks and Master Caute, he then carried it un-
scathed through that great siege, *anno* 1968, of which I
writ you an accompt at the time[1]. Which signal service he
would not let us forget; and therefore, having compleated
his paper in that famous *Black Book* on education[2], he has
now compiled a *White Book* or *album*, which is kept in the
club-room and shown to visitors. There you may see,
fully set out in documents, pictures, etc., the whole
history of that famous siege: how that great club, having
shut its gates and manned its walls, stood firm against the
barbarian hordes (being four undergraduates armed with
a banner); how Dr Rowse, by his eloquence, confounded
their arguments (see Master Lancaster's exquisite drawing
thereof, now in private hands); and how Master Warden
himself, having captured the banner in a sortie, afterwards returned it to the enemy, under flag of truce, with
privy textual emendations.

Therefore, good brother Londiniensis, lose no time, but
dedicate to Master Warden some ingeniose (but not sub-
versive) treatise: as for instance, *Of the Art of Conserving
a Commonwealth*, or *The True Modell of an University*, or
Funerary Urns, or *De Spintriis Quaestiones CXX*. Let it
be elegant in style, and forget not to intersperse a few delicate compliments, for which I trust that I have given you
matter enough in this letter; and then, with discreet commendations from myself and other sound orthodox friends,
who knows but that, by this third way, you may yet enter

---

[1] See above pp. 3–4.

[2] This must refer to the collection of articles entitled *Black Paper 2: The
Crisis in Education* which was published by the Critical Quarterly Society in
October 1969 and included a contribution by the Warden of All Souls on the
subject of 'Revolt and Reform in Oxford, 1968–69'.

that Elysian place? Where certainly no man would more gladly see you enjoying your ease than
> your loving brother to serve you,
> MERCURIUS OXONIENSIS

P.S.: I pray you, fail not to burn this letter.

XVIII

ON SIGNS AND PORTENTS

Mercurius Oxoniensis to Mercurius Londiniensis
27 June 1970

GOOD BROTHER LONDINIENSIS

Alack, alack, we are now both utterly undone! How to explain that fatall miscarriage of my long letter concerning the Old-soules club, which I directed to you with such secresy, I know not; but since Master Lawson has got his hands on it, and has publish'd it to the world, all our hopes are dash'd to the ground, and now you are no more likely to be elected to a visiting fellowship of that club than I am to be bidden to its annual collation on the day of our Encaenia, now imminent. Indeed, happy shall I be if I escape a worse fate; for 'tis reported thence that our good Dr Rowse, whom I meant only to flatter by my observations, has taken 'em so much amiss that he is now using high language against me and threatens to sue out a writ of *scandalum magnatum* for my supposed impertinency. So now I must skulk in the country, an outlaw from my college and humane society, having left strict instructions to the college porter, and to my good scout Mudge, on no accompt to accept delivery of any document, how innocent-seeming soever, which might prove to be a writ from that implacable Doctor.

But indeed, all this past se'nnight there has been nothing here but a series of ill omens. For first, on Thursday 11th June, the Provost and certain Fellows of the Queen's coll. being in solemn session in their upper common room, it pleased God to launch a fearful thunderstorm, in the course of which those worthy governours saw the great stone eagle, which sits on the pediment of their library as the embleme of their power, suddenly struck by lightning and dissolved before their eyes; after which the roof above 'em began to crack and gape, and a great body of rainwater, plaister and other *detritus* to fall upon 'em, so that 'twas only by headlong flight that that whole assembly escaped certain death; which would have been a sad loss to that society.

'Tis true, the college would not have been left quite without lawful authority, for two of its Fellows, by divine premonition, were absent from that meeting, having chosen that time to go out into the highways preaching orthodox morality; but this special favour shown to those two just men has only increased the fears of the rest of us, as seeming to vindicate those prophets who, in times past, have branded our society with the crimes, and threatened it with the chastisement, of Sodom and Gomorrah. I need not to remind you of Master Professor Kilpatrick his eloquent sermon[1] in the university church some twelve years ago (the last time he preach'd in that place); wherein he adjured the congregation (which, apart from Master Vice-chancellour, the Proctors, the bedells, etc., consisted mainly of a girls' school, brought thither by their head-mistress for edification) that that nameless vice was now so prevalent in Oxon that no undergraduate was safe from his tutor, and that fire and brimstone would infallibly descend from heaven upon us; as they have now done, even upon his own college.

[1] For Professor Kilpatrick's sermon, see the reports in the public press, 13 October 1958

Nor is this all; for only two nights later, we were affrighted (and I most particularly) by an even more dismall portent. For on 13th June, chancing to enter the great quadrangle of Christ-church in order to learn from Master Dean (our *Pontifex Maximus*) his interpretation of this prodigy, Good Lord! what should I see before me? You must know that in the centre of that court, which the late Cardinal Wolsey began and Dr Fell has since compleated, there is an elegant stone bason containing a lily-pond, stock'd with carp and goldfishes, over which hovers an exquisite *effigies*, being none other than Mercury himself, the tutelary deity of all us lesser Mercuries; which *effigies* stands poised by one great-toe upon the lips of Aeolus (as I presume), who puffs him forth on his aërial errands.

The whole is raised aloft on a stone pedestal, around which, on feast-days, a circle of fountains plays merrily in all directions, so that our nimble patron seems to be volant at once through all the elements. This delicate image is much cultivated, both in day-time, by hundreds of visitors who take pictures of the god and feed his sacred fish, and at night, by the members of that college, whose devotion is of a less formall kind: for they leap and howl around the image, and cast strange offerings into the water; and sometimes they clothe the god curiously, or paint his *pudenda* with bright colours, or crown him with a jordan or chamber-pot; and I have even seen one of her Majesty's swans swimming around him, a captive votary, wearing a black bow-tie in proper homage; which rites, or reliques of gentilism, are held to honour the god and secure his protection for that coll., as its *palladium* or guardian deity.

But now, *proh nefas*, how changed, how fall'n! For

when I entered that quadrangle, where was he, where Mercury? Instead of that graceful statue, what should I find but ruine and bareness everywhere. For the stone basis being snapt clean across, the god himself lay prone and twisted, head-downwards under the water. Truly no such omen of disaster has befallen any society since the Athenian Mercuries were so shamefully mutilated at the setting out of that great expedition to Sicily, whose sad event was thereby presaged. Of which mutilation the historian tells us that the perpetrators were not known, but commonly thought to be wild young men who feasted with Alcibiades[1]; which at least distinguishes it from this modern outrage: for I am assur'd that its authours were grave young men who that night had been hospitably entertain'd by the chaplain.

I must add that this is not the only time that this god has been barbarously used in that convivial society; for his image, having been first set up *anno* 1695, was in 1817 smash'd in pieces (the reliques are still preserv'd in the Library) by a troupe of young Mohocks led by the late earl of Derby, since prime minister (the same who so prettily english'd Homer his *Ilias*); after which the pedestal remained void for more than a hundred years, till the *lacuna* was fill'd by the present delicate statue, the gift of the late Master Bompas. 'Tis a replica of that exquisite work which the Flemish artist Master Jean de Boulogne, by some call'd Giambologna, wrought for the Grand Duke of Tuscany; and sure the originall was never more nobly placed in Florence than this copy in that Arcadian quadrangle whence it is now remov'd for repair;

[1] See Thucydides, *Peloponnesian War* VI. 27–29.

and 'tis to be hoped that we shall not wait another hundred years for his restauration.

Other strange portents have been reported in Oxon at this time: as, that it has rained blood in the Nuffield college of Psephology; that sewers have run backward to their source in Wadham coll.; and that the very stones of Balliol coll., like the statue of Memnon, have sighed and groaned at the goings-on in that place. A heifer on Port Meadow, being rounded up by my Lord Mayor (our worthy Master Maclagan of Trinity coll., the great herald, now Poursuivant Portcullis), turned and addressed him in the antient Greek tongue, not forgetting the correct accents (but in the obsolete pronunciation of the late bishop of Winton[1], so that my Lord Mayor lost some of the finer shades of meaning). 'Tis thought she prophesied (but delphically) some great mutation in our publick affairs. The entrails of a battery-fed duck, chosen for dinner on Sunday by the Provost of Oriel coll., were found, when opened, to be purple-spotted. A pullet's egg, being pierced at breakfast by the Principal of Jesus coll., cry'd out piteously, 'Free Wales!' But being offer'd full participation in all college committees, it fell silent and submitted to be eaten quietly by the Principal; etc., etc.

These are strange times, good brother Londiniensis, and I pray that no great catastrophe is to befall us. For myself, after the overthrow of the Christ-church Mercurius, in whom I had placed my trust, I have fled altogether from Oxon and have been, since Thursday

---

[1] The reference is presumably to Stephen Gardiner, Henry VIII's bishop of Winchester, who imposed his peculiar pronunciation on the university of Cambridge by penal statutes. It has since been replaced by 'the more classical pronunciation' of Erasmus.

last (since squire Todhunter is away fishing in Ireland), delitescent in Herefordshire, where I have put myself under the protection of another god, *viz*: Faunus, whom the poet calls *Mercurialium custos virorum*[1]; and till that statue be restor'd to its place, and I cleer of trouble from the Old-soules club, and assur'd that our correspondence has become inviolable, you must expect to hear no more from

your distress'd brother to serve you,

MERCURIUS OXONIENSIS

P.S.: Here in the country is no news, so I know not the issue of our generall election. The last I heard in Oxon was that Master Wilson and his crew were assur'd of victory: only the margin in doubt. The Nuffield psephologists (whose science is now declar'd by them infallible) pronounced that it would unquestionably be massive, and the Principal of St Andrews' university, being in Oxon that very day, and intimate with the great contrivers of that Party, offer'd odds of five to one. From such oracles there can be no dissent, so I assume their victory and ask only for details concerning our friends. How vast was Captain Maxwell's majority (he is squire Todhunter's member)? Is Master George Brown again of the cabinet-council? Are the Beatles yet made knights, and Sir G. Weidenfeld a baron, and my lord Annan a duke[2]?

---

[1] See Horace *Odes* ii. 17.

[2] Regrettably, the oracles were proved wrong; Mr Wilson and his party were not returned; and all these appointments and honours were thereby frustrated. This is perhaps the great mutation which the omens observed by Mercurius had portended.

99

APPENDIX

(see p. 22)

A Brief Life

R. H. Dundas, of Ch: Ch:, Oxon, was Scotch by birth, his father sheriff of Duns, Berwickshire (whence also Duns Scotus, the Subtile Doctor; but others deduce him from Embleton in Northumberland). He was bred up in England, at Eaton coll., and afterwards at New Coll., Oxon; then, for the rest of his days, Student (as they call their Fellows) at Ch: Ch. But he remained *patriae memor*, as those of that nation do, even when transplanted to more civil societies. He once went so far as to introduce haggis (a barbarous dish) to the High Table at Ch: Ch:, who rightly rejected it and never suffered it to return. He kept a fair house in Scotland, in Stirling, all his life and would invite his pupills thither in vacation. His sister made them welcome—at least such as did not guffle their soup, which she would in no wise suffer (as ———— ———— did: *quaere plus de hoc*).

As a scholler he was no great shakes. The examiners at Oxon put him in the first class, but he was not puffed up thereby. 'Twas absurd, he would say, there should be but one class for himself and Jack Beazley (Sir J. B., the great pot-critick). He was a Grecian, taught the history of the Greeks, and especially their diseases (clap, haemorrhoids, etc.), to which he ascribed much of their publick acts; but in general he despised deep researches, holding to the good old view that dons should drink port and mind the boyes, as he did himself, perhaps too much. In the second of our great warres he lost his notes, wherefrom he taught; which loss (occasioned by some misdirection by the publick carrier) mightily discouraged him. It was magnified by his pupills (*Mem.* never believe undergraduates), until some supposed that a *magnum opus* had perished; but 'twas only a parcel of old jottings made by himself as an undergraduate, filled out with trifles.

He served in the first warre in Mesopotamia and corresponded almost daily with the Lady Mary Murray; who however afterwards, in a huff, sent back all his letters. The reason unknown: some suppose that he had grumped to her (as he did to others) that her husband, Gilbert Murray, then Regius Professor of Greek (and so of Ch: Ch:), would not join in college port-bibbing; which she, being a furious water-drinker, no doubt resented. N.B. She was the daughter of that Countess of Carlisle who emptied his Lordship's claret into the moat at Naworth: a horrid fact.

Returning to Ch: Ch:, he held the office of Censor, which he prized mightily. Would say that once a man had been censor of Ch: Ch: there was nothing left for him to do: 'twas the *acme* or zenith of human life. He maintained that he was the best censor that coll. had ever had; which others doubted. He had a mysticall notion of the censorship, not shared by his successors, on whom he made sharp animadversions, as they on him; but 'tis a matter of opinion only.

He had a dry, laconicall way of expressing himself, more apophthegmaticall than profound, but useful to rebuke the impertinency of youth. His correspondence was terse, by post-card. He also wrote comments on undergraduates, grading 'em like cattle, *alpha, beta, gamma*, whether plump or no, pink-faced or exsuccous, etc. These comments he writ in a neat, exiguous hand on backs of envelopes, which he would then preserve (his rooms a very jackdaw's nest) and bring up thirty years later to disconcert 'em.

Appendix

He was *Paederastes*, but Platonick: assured the world he was a virgin *quoad corpus*: at most a viewer. He would question the young men curiously, and *de pudendis*; which they, being ingenuous youths, and forewarned by their fellows, took in good part. Sometimes, I fear, they pulled the old boy's leg. One only took it amiss and complained to his parents, and they to others, and so it was objected to him; whereupon he, in umbrage, took leave of absence for a year and sailed round the world, viewing naked boys, brown, black and yellow, diving for sponges etc.; which pleased him mightily. His other observations on the world were very trivial (no cosmopolite, no delight in art or letters). Then he returned to his old tricks, and viewed again in Parson's Pleasure.

He would visit schools also, for the same purpose, till deflected by headmasters, and would give passage in his car to stable-boys, who told him of strange doings in the bedstraw of Lambourn and Newmarket (*quaere,*whether unsollicited?). On Friday nights he would—as allowed by the rules of that society—invite youths from other colls. to the High Table of Ch: Ch: and question them over the snuff. Would sometimes, when *inter pocula*, forget himself. I have heard him quiz one of His late Majesty's learned judges, whether circumciz'd or no. I forget the judge's answer.

These curious indagations he somehow persuaded himself were right and useful: a publick duty wrongly neglected by others and left to him, as alone sustaining antique morality. 'Tis marvellous how men deceive themselves about their own motives; for I would impute hypocrisy to no man.

He was generous and would do good by stealth. By his

105

prying, how impertinent soever, he would sometimes discover the needs of the young men, and privately relieve them, or see them relieved; which won him gratitude and caused all his faults (which at worst were venial) to be forgotten.

He believed—'tis the *naeve* of Ch: Ch: men—that Ch: Ch: was the centre of the world. He kept its annual record, marvellously complete (he had the eye of a hawk for detail) and maintained all the old traditions, sometimes adding new: e.g. that of emptying the residue of the port-decanter into his own glass as unfit for keeping; which did no good to his liver.

He died in Edinburgh, *anno* 1960, *aetatis suae* 76. After his death there was much ado to recover a curious illustrated book which he had borrowed (through a Minister of the Kirk) from a Scotch noblewoman, and not yet returned. 'Twas run down at last, in the hands of a fellow collegian, like him a batchelour. 'Tis now safe in Bodley's library, reserved to be read only by Heads of Houses, Bishops, etc. 'Tis best in such hands, for 'tis of rare indecency.

His life has now been writ by Master Roger Venables, and is printed by Sir B. Blackwell, in octavo, and to be bought at his shop in Broad-street; but 'tis very taedious. The lives of these old collegians should be writ briefly. Theirs are vegetable virtues, to be distilled, not dilated, and without a grain of salt hardly to be saved from insipidity. 'Twould have tickled the old rogue to see himself eterniz'd in this bumbling litany. But 'tis a work of piety, so let it pass.

JOHN AUBREY, F.R.S.